DEVELOPING A LOVE OF READING AND BOOKS

Sara Miller McCune founded SAGE Publishing in 1965 to support the dissemination of usable knowledge and educate a global community. SAGE publishes more than 1000 journals and over 800 new books each year, spanning a wide range of subject areas. Our growing selection of library products includes archives, data, case studies and video. SAGE remains majority owned by our founder and after her lifetime will become owned by a charitable trust that secures the company's continued independence.

Los Angeles | London | New Delhi | Singapore | Washington DC | Melbourne

DEVELOPING A LOVE OF READING AND BOOKS

TEACHING AND NURTURING READERS IN PRIMARY SCHOOLS

ANGELA GILL
MEGAN STEPHENSON
DAVID WAUGH

Learning Matters
A SAGE Publishing Company

Learning Matters
A SAGE Publishing Company
1 Oliver's Yard
55 City Road
London EC1Y 1SP

SAGE Publications Inc.
2455 Teller Road
Thousand Oaks, California 91320

SAGE Publications India Pvt Ltd
B 1/I 1 Mohan Cooperative Industrial Area
Mathura Road
New Delhi 110 044

SAGE Publications Asia-Pacific Pte Ltd
3 Church Street
#10-04 Samsung Hub
Singapore 049483

Editor: Amy Thornton
Senior project editor: Chris Marke
Marketing manager: Lorna Patkai
Cover design: Wendy Scott
Typeset by: C&M Digitals (P) Ltd, Chennai, India
Printed in the UK

First edition published by Learning Matters/
SAGE 2021

Library of Congress Control Number: 2020945716

British Library Cataloguing in Publication Data

A catalogue record for this book is available from the
British Library.

ISBN 978-1-5297-3000-5
ISBN 978-1-5297-2999-3 (pbk)

At SAGE we take sustainability seriously. Most of our products are printed in the UK using responsibly sourced
papers and boards. When we print overseas we ensure sustainable papers are used as measured by the
PREPS grading system. We undertake an annual audit to monitor our sustainability.

Contents

Contents

Acknowledgements

Lucy M. Davies would like to thank John Emmerson Batty Primary School in Redcar, in particular, Julie Norris and Rebecca Walker for sharing their experiences.

Catherine Lenahan With thanks to Angela Gill, Jane Kennedy and Kerry Coates for encouragement and ongoing discussion about reading environments and all things literacy.

In memory of a wonderful friend and colleague, Lynn Thompson. A truly inspirational teacher.

About the editors and contributors

The editors

Angela Gill is an assistant professor at Durham University. She is the Curriculum and Student Experience Lead of the UG and PGCE ITE programmes in the School of Education and is the Subject Lead for Primary English. For more than twenty years, Angela taught in primary schools in Durham and Somerset, during which time she was Subject Lead for English and phonics. She has written and edited books and articles about many aspects of Primary English. Her most recent publications include the 3rd edition of *Teaching Systematic Synthetic Phonics in Primary Schools,* which she co-wrote with Wendy Jolliffe and David Waugh, and *Mastering Writing at Greater Depth,* for which she was an editor and chapter author.

Megan Stephenson is a senior lecturer in English and PGCE Primary Phase Co-ordinator in the Primary Education Department at Leeds Trinity University. She teaches English on both the undergraduate and postgraduate ITT programmes. She has taught in six primary schools in Leeds and Bradford over the last 25 years, where she has led both the Reading Recovery and phonics teaching – including the training of staff within the Local Education Authority. Megan has contributed to several books focusing on the value of creative learning environments in order to develop a love of learning. Her most recent publication includes a chapter entitled Developing Deeper Writing in KS1 Through the Use of High-quality Texts, in *Mastering Writing at Greater Depth*. She has presented at National Conferences in the UK on her approach to developing 'Inspirational Teacher Education', and is currently writing further material exemplifying the benefits of vocabulary-rich early years settings.

David Waugh is Professor of Education at Durham University. He has published extensively in primary English. David is a former deputy head teacher and was Head of the Education Department at the University of Hull and Regional Adviser for ITT for the National Strategies from 2008 to 2010. He has written and co-written or edited more than 40 books on primary education. As well as his educational writing, David also writes children's stories and regularly teaches in schools. In 2017, he wrote *The Wishroom* with 45 children from fifteen East Durham Schools and recently completed *Twins?*, working with twelve Year 5–6 pupils.

The contributors

Teresa Cremin is Professor of Education (Literacy) at the Open University. An ex-teacher, staff development co-ordinator and ITE tutor, Teresa now undertakes research and consultancy in the UK and abroad. Her research focuses on volitional reading and writing, teachers' literate identities and practices and creative pedagogies. She has published very widely in these areas; her most recent text is *Children Reading for Pleasure in the Digital Age: Mapping Reader Engagement* (with N. Kucirkova, 2019). Teresa is passionate about developing readers for life and leads a practitioner website based on her research into reading for pleasure. The site supports OU/UKLA Teachers' Reading Groups and HEI partnerships to enable the development of children's and teachers' reading for pleasure. https://ourfp.org/

Cathy Lawson is a lecturer in English and Professional Studies in the Institute of Childhood and Education at Leeds Trinity University (LTU). She has been involved in initial teacher education for sixteen years. She led the English department at Bradford College for eleven years and is currently the Level 4 Co-ordinator at LTU. Her work in higher education has been influenced by thirteen years of teaching and management experience in various schools in Bradford. Catherine particularly enjoys mentoring trainee teachers in school and has taken on this role throughout her career. Catherine is currently involved in research regarding the teaching of grammar and punctuation in primary schools.

Samantha Wilkes is a lecturer in English across both undergraduate and postgraduate trainees at Leeds Trinity University. She is Level 5 Phase Co-ordinator and leads the Early Years English programmes in the Primary Education Department, ITT. Leading up to this she has worked across differing primary schools in Leeds and Bradford, spanning over two decades, and has worked in senior roles: as Deputy Head and Head of School.

She has a specialism across Early Years English and consultation experience with senior leaders in nurseries and schools with engaging learners, smooth transition to Year 1 and developing and fostering a love of books, reading and writing. She is currently involved in presenting at the University of Leeds, Research Workshop on Language Development and Children Learning Adjectives.

Rachel Rudman is a senior lecturer at Leeds Trinity University where she leads the secondary English PGCE and supervises dissertations for the Masters in Education course. Previously, she taught in secondary schools across Yorkshire, with experience which culminated in leading an English department. Rachel works with one of the main examination boards and leads on assessment of English Language A level and has delivered training and produced examination reports for schools nationwide on the examination. She has previously contributed to two books, one of which focused on A level English Language as a whole and another which was entitled *Language Development*.

Lucy M. Davies MA (Education) is an assistant professor in Humanities in primary education in the School of Education at Durham University. Her research interests are in engagement in learning and in creative thinking. She has presented her research at conferences in England

and Europe and was a researcher on the Durham Commission on Creativity (2019), a cross-curricular project in the University in association with Arts Council England.

Steve Higgins is Professor of Education at Durham University. He is a former primary school teacher and has a particular interest in discourse and interaction in classrooms, the use of digital technologies for teaching and learning and the use of evidence to improve education. He is the lead author of the Education Endowment Foundation's Teaching and Learning Toolkit. He has written widely on education for academic, policy and practitioner audiences.

Fay Lewis is a senior lecturer in STEM Education and Programme Lead for the MA Education at UWE Bristol. Before moving into higher education Fay taught in primary schools in East Yorkshire, Bristol and Somerset for over fifteen years, during which time she was Subject Lead for maths and science. She has published works relating to many aspects of primary STEM, including maths, engineering and science.

Rachel Simpson is an Assistant Professor at Durham University. She is the Deputy Director of Professional Programmes at the School of Education and is the Subject Lead for Primary Science. Rachel taught extensively in primary schools in Cambridgeshire before moving to Vietnam to teach in an international school. Her areas of interest include effective use of formative assessment in both the primary classroom and higher education, and the development of teachers' creative thinking skills.

Jo Smith is an assistant professor at Durham University. She co-leads the secondary PGCE programme for science as a physics specialist, teaches Constructivism and Science Misconceptions at Masters level and has taught various undergraduate ITE modules, including Science, Early Years and Design and Technology at the School of Education. Jo has teaching experience in both secondary and primary schools, having taught from Early Years to A Level, with subject lead roles in Science, Early Years and Arts across schools and school federations being held. This is her first book chapter, and she hopes there will be more to come.

David Whitehead is the ITE University–Schools Partnership Lead for the undergraduate and postgraduate ITE programmes at the Centre for Education, Durham University. David has over twenty years' experience of teaching in primary schools in England during which time he mentored numerous trainees and newly qualified teachers.

Christina Castling is a playwright, drama facilitator and teacher trainer based in County Durham (www.christinacastling.co.uk). She has been delivering drama and creative writing projects within schools for ten years and is the founder of Off The Page Drama CIC. She regularly works with a variety of cultural and educational organisations, including Live

Theatre, New Writing North and The Forge, and particularly enjoys helping teachers develop their confidence in using creativity in the classroom.

Charlotte Wright is a senior lecturer in Education and Programme Co-ordinator for the MA in Education at Leeds Trinity University. She has taught English for 25 years in a range of schools, trained new teachers in the Department of Education at Oxford University and continues to teach in a Leeds school once a week. She is currently engaged in a doctorate in Education looking at the theorising practice of English teachers. She has published work in NATE's *English Drama Media* magazine and speaks at local and national conferences on issues relating to English teaching and teacher training.

Diana Mann is a senior lecturer in Professional Studies for the Primary Education Department at Leeds Trinity University. She teaches a range of modules covering aspects of Professional Studies, including safeguarding and inclusion, across the undergraduate and postgraduate ITT programmes. She taught in six primary schools in the Leeds area and before moving into ITT at Leeds Trinity University in 2015, was a primary school head teacher for eighteen years in three different schools, all in challenging circumstances. Diana completed an MA in supporting children with English as an additional language (MA EALE) to fulfil their learning potential in school and has contributed to the NALDIC *EAL Journal*. The education of vulnerable primary school-aged children, particularly those from deprived backgrounds, those who are asylum seekers/refugees or those within diverse families, is an area of particular focus.

Amanda Nuttall is a senior lecturer in Primary Education at Leeds Trinity University, where she leads undergraduate Initial Teacher Education provision. Prior to working in ITE, Amanda taught for thirteen years in primary schools in Leeds and surrounding areas. She is currently undertaking DPhil study at the University of Oxford. Her research is focused on understanding how teachers experience identity changes when they engage in Masters level research activity. This research focus is influenced by her own experiences as a research-active teacher in disadvantaged schools, alongside her recent work in developing research literacy for student teachers.

Kulwinder Maude recently took up a post at Durham University, as an assistant professor in primary English, after five years as senior lecturer at Kingston University, London. She has over twenty years of experience working in different sectors of education (both UK and India). She teaches English on undergraduate and postgraduate initial teacher education programmes along with teaching on Masters level modules on reflective teaching and issues linked with inclusion. Her research interests are primarily focused on key issues in teaching and pedagogy of primary English, with a special interest in English as an additional language. She has written articles and chapters on many aspects of primary English and EAL for ITE and primary practitioners.

Stefan Kucharczyk is the founder of *ARTiculate Education*, which offers consultancy on creative writing for primary schools and creative writing and film workshops for children. Stefan has more than ten years' experience working in primary and higher education. He has written on many aspects of creativity and children's literacy. He is currently writing a book about teaching Shakespeare for primary literacy in the 21st century (due 2021). He leads the Teacher Talking Time listening project, interviewing primary practitioners about their experiences (www.teachertalkingtime.co.uk).

Links:

articulateeducation@gmail.com
www.articulateeducation.co.uk
www.teachertalkingtime.co.uk

Catherine Lenahan is an independent educator adviser who is currently developing *The Map* phonics comic series. Having taught and acted as a literacy subject co-ordinator for twelve years in Durham and Hampshire local authorities, Catherine went on to work for National Strategies as a communication, language and literacy development consultant. Following five years specialising in literacy and phonics, she was an employed as an education adviser for Durham County Council providing specialist advice to primary schools and settings. Since transferring to independent advisory work, Catherine has provided ongoing consultancy advice to Education Development Trust and Hachette UK. She regularly acts as a guest lecturer for the Durham University, is a writer of phonics readings schemes and supports a number of local primary schools with a focus on Early Years and primary literacy. Her passion in life is supporting the ongoing development of children's reading skills.

Foreword

I love reading and I love books. I love the way they smell and feel. I love the journeys that they take me on. I love the escapism and the reality that they offer. But why should we help children develop this same love? In this book, the authors seek to answer that question in all of its various forms. They examine a range of advantages, from developing an understanding of diversity and inclusion in the classroom and beyond to the use of books across the various subjects of the primary curriculum. This book makes essential reading for student teachers, NQTs, RQTs and those with a vast teaching experience as it demonstrates the immensely powerful tool that is a love of reading in a variety of ways.

For me, developing a love of reading and of books is the most important thing we can do as primary school teachers. It is through books that children can learn about what it feels like to be someone else. Reading allows children to climb inside the minds of others and find out what they are thinking and why. To put it basically, reading teaches children empathy. It teaches children to look at things from other people's points of view. It is through books that children begin to make sense of the world around them and far away from them. In my opinion, teaching children to be empathic towards other human beings is the greatest gift we can impart to them, and reading books is the best way to achieve this.

The other great power of learning a love of reading and books is that it develops children's imaginations. They can discover what it is like to receive a letter from Hogwarts or to go on a bear hunt. Once they have read, or had read to them, a book about something that they have never encountered before then this new thing is part of their imagination. Books help children to discover strange and extraordinary creatures, objects and places that they may not have heard of before, from unicorns to magic keys, to a witch's hut on chicken's legs. But they can also discover equally bizarre things that truly exist in our world, like blob fishes and Venus fly traps.

As a writer, I need to read. Reading and writing are symbiotic. I think of reading as breathing in and writing as breathing out. There cannot be one without the other. So, if we want children to write well then we need them to read well. This book shows how we can inspire children to *want* to read, which will then lead them to *want* to write.

Adam Bushnell
Author and teacher

Introduction

Why does a love of reading matter?

Angela Gill, Megan Stephenson and David Waugh

National Curriculum objective

6.3 Teachers should develop pupils' reading and writing in all subjects to support their acquisition of knowledge. Pupils should be taught to read fluently, understand extended prose (both fiction and non-fiction) and be encouraged to read for pleasure. Schools should do everything to promote wider reading. They should provide library facilities and set ambitious expectations for reading at home (DfE, 2013, p10).

The 2014 English National Curriculum (DfE, 2013) was welcomed by many educators because it included a strong emphasis on reading for pleasure, an element which many felt had been neglected in previous versions. This book sets out to illustrate not only the value of reading for pleasure, but also the ways in which a culture of reading for pleasure can be developed.

In a book titled *Developing a Love of Reading and Books* you should expect to find practical guidance underpinned by case studies and research evidence to support you to achieve the aim of our subtitle: *Teaching and Nurturing Readers in Primary Schools*. We feel that, by assembling a group of experts, all of whom have considerable teaching experience and an abundance of practical ideas for the classroom, we have met the challenge we set out achieve.

Besides finding references to key research and case studies of classroom activity, you will find tips, in the concluding chapter, on how you can implement the ideas our authors describe in your own classroom. Activities have been included to reinforce understanding and to encourage you to consider what you have seen and done in schools. Each chapter indicates the elements of the Teachers' Standards (DfE, 2011) and English National Curriculum

(DfE, 2013) which are relevant to the content. You will also find recommended reading and suggestions for children's literature which you might use in the classroom.

In Chapter 1, drawing on her seminal research into reading for pleasure, Teresa Cremin explores the key elements which need to be put in place in order to develop communities of readers. She argues that enjoyment in reading is central to the culture and ethos of the classroom and will be sustained by interactive and reciprocal reader relationships. The vital importance of teachers being readers themselves with a good knowledge of texts is emphasised in a chapter which describes the key features of reading for pleasure communities.

In Chapter 2, Cathy Lawson, Samantha Wilkes and Megan Stephenson explore how the demands of a curriculum-heavy content can be met through the creative planning, teaching and delivery of engaging material. The authors draw on the previous research explored by Teresa Cremin and demonstrate how reading cultures can be established from the earliest days in Foundation Stage and throughout Key Stage 1. They go on to consider how instructional teaching of systematic synthetic phonics (SSP) can be expertly balanced with the introduction of high-quality texts that engage children and help develop a culture of and a thirst for reading.

Rachel Rudman highlights a range of ways in which to promote enjoyment of reading in the classroom and beyond in Chapter 3. Rachel explores ways in which children's reading can be nurtured through the use of challenging texts as they move into upper Key Stage 2 and looks at how a reading culture can be preserved in the transition from primary to secondary school.

Lucy M. Davies argues, in Chapter 4, that cross-curricular texts can not only develop children's subject-specific knowledge, but also their sense of individual and collective identity. Lucy maintains that literature can provide a safe and sensitive stimulus to discuss emotive topics, particularly in history, religious education and citizenship. The themes of 'creative reading' and 'critical reading' are examined in a chapter which demonstrates how art and humanities subjects provide a context for enhancing different types of reading skills.

In Chapter 5, Steve Higgins, Fay Lewis, Rachel Simpson, Jo Smith and David Whitehead maintain that using stories within science, technology, engineering and mathematics (STEM) can both encourage the act of reading and inspire pupils to improve their knowledge about scientific phenomena, the world of technology and mathematics. Practical examples of how reading can be integrated with science, technology and mathematics are provided, as well as guidance on how to develop your knowledge about reading in the wider curriculum.

In Chapter 6, Christina Castling and Charlotte Wright argue that drama and poetry can bring language to life in the classroom and show our pupils how its power can be explored and enjoyed in a range of ways. There is practical guidance on ways to create a safe and affirmative classroom where children feel happy to perform, as well as on how you can build your confidence in helping your pupils to explore the spoken word through poetry and drama. Through case studies, Christina and Charlotte show how poetry and drama can provide opportunities to learn about language through play with words, voices and audiences.

Diana Mann and Amanda Nuttall suggest, in Chapter 7, that books could be our most powerful tool for building diversity, inclusion and acceptance in our classrooms. They maintain that we have a responsibility to think carefully about the books we share with our children, ensuring authentic representation of a range of diverse, multidimensional characters. In a chapter which is highly relevant to today's society, Diana and Amanda provide tips on choosing high-quality inclusive books which ensure all children are represented in the books we read, including those which challenge stereotypes and normalise difference.

The theme of inclusivity is taken up by Kulwinder Maude in Chapter 8, where she argues that as more and more teachers find themselves teaching students from increasingly diverse linguistic and cultural backgrounds, it is vital that English for speakers of other languages (ESOL) pupils are given opportunities to engage with language through meaningful contexts where they can refine their initial thoughts through classroom talk. Kulwinder examines the key issues associated with learning to read in a second language, and looks at how we can encourage deeper reading through dual language books and use of first language.

Chapter 9, by Angela Gill, Stefan Kucharczyk and Catherine Lenahan, considers what it means to become literate in the 21st century and how the texts we encounter may go beyond books. The chapter explores some of the rewards of teaching film in primary literacy and provides strategies for teaching children to read a film. Angela, Stefan and Catherine maintain that, in a multimodal era, the inclusion of a diverse range of accessible media such as film, in the reading environment and in our teaching, can develop children's literacy skills and their levels of engagement, influence reading for meaning and contribute to the development of a love of books. In a chapter which echoes a theme from Teresa Cremin's opening chapter, the authors show why the adult role is essential to reading for meaning within any reading environment.

The final section of the book offers further support when reflecting on your own practice. It provides ideas about how you can develop a culture of reading in your classroom and the whole school. *Top Tips* are provided by our authors when implementing the ideas they describe in their chapters. These are accompanied by recommendations for further reading, children's texts, websites and high-quality resources.

We hope that by reading this book you will be stimulated to develop your knowledge and understanding of children's literature, including poetry, plays and multimodal texts.

We hope, too, that you will recognise the importance of developing a reading for pleasure culture in your classroom and beyond, sharing your own enthusiasm for reading with the children you teach.

Angela Gill
Megan Stephenson
David Waugh
March 2021

References

Department for Education (DfE) (2011) *Teachers' Standards*. Available at: https://www.gov.uk/government/publications/teachers-standards (accessed 28 July 2020).

Department for Education (2013) *The National Curriculum in England: Key Stages 1 and 2 Framework Document*. Available at: https://www.gov.uk/government/publications/national-curriculum-in-england-primary-curriculum (accessed 30 April 2020).

1 Building Communities of Engaged Readers

Teresa Cremin

Learning outcomes

By reading this chapter you will have considered:

- why it is important to build a community of engaged readers;
- the key features of such reading for pleasure (RfP) communities;
- why teachers' knowledge of texts and RfP pedagogy is central;
- how you can build a community of children who love reading.

Teachers' Standards

3. Demonstrate good subject and curriculum knowledge:

- have a secure knowledge of the relevant subject(s) and curriculum areas, foster and maintain pupils' interest in the subject;
- demonstrate an understanding of and take responsibility for promoting high standards of literacy and articulacy.

Curriculum link

6.3 Teachers should develop pupils' reading and writing in all subjects to support their acquisition of knowledge. Pupils should be taught to read fluently, understand extended prose (both fiction and non-fiction) and be encouraged to read for pleasure. Schools should do everything to promote wider reading. They should provide library facilities and set ambitious expectations for reading at home (DfE, 2013, p10).

Introduction

Reading may be undertaken by individual readers, but it is a highly social practice. Your attitude to reading and the pleasure or otherwise you take in it, has been influenced by your reading history and the ways your teachers at school viewed you as a reader, and your experiences. Countless biographies attest to the fact that those around us (and this includes the authors and editors of the books, magazines and newspapers we read) shape our reading lives and impact on the kind of readers we are and might become. Given that reading for pleasure in childhood is a highly influential factor in children's future academic success (Sullivan and Brown, 2015) and also impacts on their well-being, as argued in Chapter 4, then offering social support for young readers in school is essential. Building communities of engaged readers is, therefore, not an optional extra; it is essential to develop a love of reading and ensure that children who can read, actually choose to do so.

In this chapter, drawing on my research into reading for pleasure (Cremin *et al.*, 2014), I explore the key elements which need to be put in place in order to develop communities of readers. These are summarised in Figure 1.1 and reveal that professional knowledge of children's texts, and of readers, an RfP pedagogy (encompassing reading aloud, independent reading time and book talk and reading recommendations in a highly social environment) and being a Reading Teacher (a teacher who reads and a reader who teaches) are key. These four elements combine to construct communities in which there are strong relationships between

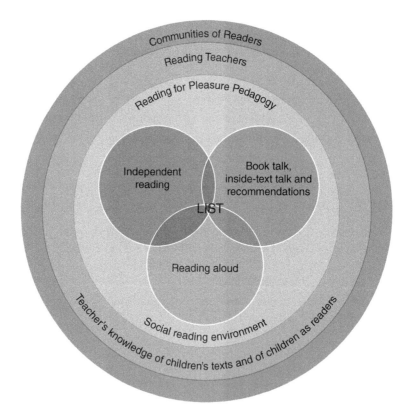

Figure 1.1   Research insights regarding the effective development of reading for pleasure (based on Cremin et al., 2014)

teachers and children, and children and children around reading. Such communities are characterised by reciprocity and interaction. They take time to build, and shift reading from being an individual private pursuit to a more collaborative social activity.

Each of the elements shown in Figure 1.1 is examined in this chapter, illuminated by case studies of schools and classrooms which have successfully built vibrant communities of readers. Some schools have also blurred the boundaries to encompass parents and the wider community. Communities are not static, however, and are arguably never fully 'achieved'; they need constant nurturing, such that teachers continue to widen their knowledge of contemporary children's texts, get to know their children better as readers and redouble their efforts to ensure their RfP pedagogy is LIST – Learner-led, Informal, Social and with Texts that Tempt. Teachers also need to constantly consider their own reading practices, as this can enable them to participate as thoughtful and socially interactive readers, not just pedagogues. Building communities of readers is essential in order to support children's pleasure in reading.

Empty demonstrations of community need to be avoided, through the investment in new libraries, the purchasing of double-decker buses as libraries, tents, sheds and reading corners which showcase a school's commitment to reading, but are then neither timetabled nor used to support readers. Cushions and sofas don't make readers, nor do reading competitions and the writing of endless book reviews! Professional subject knowledge of texts and of real children and rich practice is key if you wish children to become readers for life – readers who choose what to read and read at their own pace, in their own way and for their own purposes.

Teachers' knowledge of texts and children as readers

Teachers' knowledge of texts and of readers is the cornerstone on which interactive communities of readers are built (Cremin, 2019a). Teachers need to have wide and deep repertoires of children's literature *and* get to know the interests and practices of the young readers in their classes. This enables teachers to skilfully book-match and tailor recommendations to particular individuals, ensuring relevant and interesting texts are offered and young people are not merely left on their own to choose. Informed professional support is needed. Teachers have a social and moral responsibility to keep up to date with contemporary children's books, as well as a strong working knowledge of the 'old and gold' from yesteryear. In addition, knowledge of a range of genres is needed and awareness of texts which reflect the realities of all learners.

There are myriad ways of broadening this vital subject knowledge, including for example: reading award winners, such as those of the Carnegie, Kate Greenaway, Blue Peter, Costa, School Library Association and UK Literacy Association (UKLA) awards; accepting the 52-book challenge by reading a book a week; or reading beyond one's comfort zone and exploring graphic novels, poetry, verse novels or children's non-fiction, for instance. Many teachers also make their own library shelf in the classroom, showcasing the books they have read and can now discuss and share with children. These tend to become popular books as conversations about them engage children, promoting further reading by that author and often enabling two-way reciprocal recommendations between teachers and children. These 'books in common' often trigger the sharing of life connections and help nurture new relationships between adults and children.

Developing knowledge of individual children's interests, home reading practices, preferences and identities is also crucial. This can be undertaken through surveys, reading histories or making 24-hour reads (collages of all that that was read across the time frame) or 'reading rivers' (documenting the diversity of everyday reading experiences but perhaps over a longer time period). Such information when analysed and combined with records of children's reading choices and preferences enables teachers to build reader-to-reader relationships and connect children to others in the class who also find gritty emotional stories or comics engaging, for instance. Over time, when appropriately supported by well-read teachers, children will begin to exchange texts with one another and waiting lists for books will be established, serving to raise interest and develop desire. It is important to recognise the value of these emerging reader-to-reader networks and commit to sustaining them.

Research focus

The Teachers as Readers (TaRs) (Phase 1) research showed that teachers' knowledge of children's literature is dominated by Dahl, by other 'celebrity' authors and by the books that they read in childhood. This inadequate subject knowledge is insufficient to support the development of young readers (Cremin et al., 2008, 2014). A National Literacy Trust survey undertaken in 2015 found little had changed, the results were very similar: teachers relied on a narrow range of children's authors and Dahl was pre-eminent (Clark and Teravainen, 2017). In addition, the Centre for Literacy in Primary Education (2019), in highlighting the paucity of black and minority ethnic (BAME) characters in children's literature, found that only 7 per cent of books published in 2018 in the UK contained a BAME character, yet a third of UK school-age children are 'of minority ethnic origins' (DfE, 2018). It is vital therefore that teachers seek out such texts as they widen their repertoires. Books act as mirrors enabling children to see their lives reflected in what they read, and as doors and windows on the wider world, enabling them to develop empathy, tolerance and understanding of others' situations. Time-pressed teachers often turn to digital library systems to help them make book recommendations to children, but these tend to position teachers as librarians, curators and monitors of children's reading, and can create a surveillance culture. This undermines teachers' potential roles as listeners, mentors and co-readers, which have been shown to positively impact on children's pleasure in reading (Kucirkova and Cremin, 2020).

Activity

To establish your strengths and areas for development in relation to children's literature and other texts, you will want to audit your subject knowledge. Go to the Open University's (OU's) reading for pleasure site, based on Teresa Cremin's research, and download the 'Review your practice' document focused on this:

https://www.researchrichpedagogies.org/research/theme/teachers-knowledge-of-childrens-literature-and-other-texts

Having completed this self-review document, consider:

- What do you feel most confident about?
- What areas were you less knowledgeable about?
- Look up some of the authors you named – when did they last publish a book?
- To what extent are the authors or books you named focused on offering texts which reflect BAME voices and views?

Set yourself a reading challenge – see the suggestions above and share what you read with the children in your class.

Case study

In Elmhurst Primary School in Newham, London, Kat Young and Clara Breakwell have been leading a whole-school initiative to enrich staff knowledge of children's literature and their RfP pedagogy over several years. The school, which is one of the DfE English hubs focused on developing a love of reading, as the third aim of the hubs, alongside high-quality phonics provision and the enrichment of children's vocabulary.

In order to achieve this, all staff undertook the OU staff audit of their subject knowledge of children's texts and this helped them identify areas for development. As Jonny Walker (2017) from the school later wrote:

> most primary teachers are still laymen when it comes to children's fiction. We endorse and celebrate the same small few authors who we read ourselves as children. We read the pupils the same small group of books that they are most likely to access at home. At the moment, this would be Dahl and Walliams.

In order to widen staff knowledge, Kat set up a staff book club. This met on a Friday after school in a local café once per half term to discuss an adult book and a children's book. Attendance was good; many staff unable to go each time committed to reading the agreed books, which prompted staffroom conversations and increased sharing with children. Staff were also given money to buy books as Christmas presents for children in their classes and these nudged teachers to get to know their children and select appropriate texts from their wider repertoires.

The staff book group later became an OU/UKLA Teachers' Reading Group, one of over 200 across the country that have been run since 2018 linked to the OU's research-informed website (Cremin et al., 2014). Do consider joining one and check out the details on the site: https://ourfp.org/. The groups aim to foster children's reading for pleasure through supporting members' own RfP and research-informed practice and build professional RfP communities locally and online. Members share their resultant development work on the website. In 2019, Elmhurst Primary School won the Egmont Reading for Pleasure Award (launched with the OU and UKLA) in the whole-school category. Read their case study on creating a culture of RfP with teachers' knowledge of children's texts at its heart here: https://www.researchrichpeda gogies.org/research/example/creating-a-culture-of-reading-for-pleasure

This case study highlights that if teachers recognise their responsibility to develop their subject knowledge of children's literature and other texts, they begin to share a newfound passion for reading. As Frank Cottrell Boyce, the children's author, has observed, 'we cannot teach pleasure in reading, but we can share it' (quoted in Cremin et al., 2014). This professional pleasure in turn serves to shape a more effective RfP pedagogy.

RfP pedagogy

Developing a rigorous, evidence-informed RfP pedagogy is important, as simply engaging in random 'fun' reading activities is ineffective in supporting readers, as HMI Sarah Hubbard from Ofsted (2019) noted. Reading aloud, reading time, book talk and recommendations in social reading environments are key elements of the wider reading curriculum and deserve to be timetabled and carefully planned and evaluated. The effectiveness of this RfP pedagogy relies upon teachers' subject knowledge and knowledge of their children, and professional understanding of reading, as social, relational and affectively engaging. Endorsed by the NUT (2016), this fourfold pedagogy needs to be embedded into practice and sustained over time. As noted earlier, the RfP pedagogy checkLIST helps teachers plan to ensure activities are Learner-led, Informal, Social and with Texts that Tempt the young people themselves (Cremin and Durning, 2020).

In relation to reading aloud, for instance, the National Curriculum is clear, stating that 'pupils should continue to have opportunities to listen frequently to stories, poems, nonfiction and other writing, including whole books and not just extracts, so that they build on what was taught previously' (DfE, 2013, p38). This is important as nearly 10 per cent of children aged eight to eighteen years in England have no books at home (Clark and Teravainen, 2017), and once children have learnt to read parents tend to stop reading to them (Merga and Ledger, 2018). The quality of the texts that are sent home often does not help, however; many motivate neither the child nor the parent. Parental support and engaging texts are needed. Many schools offer support by sending toy animals and sachets of hot chocolate for young children and their parents to enjoy, hoping to trigger a 'cuddle up with a book at bedtime'. Others offer staff read-alouds on the school website, and still others loan audiobooks.

Schools also need to devote time to reading aloud for children aged five to eleven years and beyond. Hearing engaging texts read aloud well is highly motivating; it offers an external model of reading in the head and prompts children to process more challenging texts and vocabulary than they could possibly achieve on their own. Significantly too, when books are shared, read and re-read in ways that involve teachers, siblings, parents and grandparents, then family or class 'books in common' are created. These create bonds between those who share the experience of the text and engage in discussions about it. Talk can play a key part in reading aloud as readers make text-to-life and life-to-text connections, in order to explore the text's meaning and their response. This is not, however, a comprehension exercise led by the teachers, but a motivated and affective reflection upon what it offers to each reader.

Research focus

As a large-scale study has shown, reading aloud frequently to four- to five-year-olds enhances children's reading, maths and cognitive skills at age eight to nine years (Kalb and van Ours, 2013), and in the early primary years teachers' book promotions and children's choice-led 'book shopping' from classroom baskets can develop their desire to read (Moses and Kelly, 2018). Additionally, as the Teachers as Readers (Phase 2) research showed (with children from five to 11 years) books which we live through together for the sole purpose of shared enjoyment represent a rich resource for conversation, for connection and for spinning webs of reader relationships (Cremin *et al.*, 2014). Such 'books in common' nurture our pleasure in reading and play a particularly resonant role in helping build communities of engaged readers. Learning from this three-year study, it is important to note that it is not whether teachers read aloud that counts, or indeed whether they offer an independent reading time, critically it is *how* these opportunities are shaped and lived. Both can easily become routinised periods when children choose to switch off from listening or merely flick at the pages of a book imposed upon them.

Positive opportunities for children to read aloud also need to be mapped into the wider reading curriculum – for example, through the creation of 'reading buddies' from different year groups and/or with reading volunteers; or reading to each other in small groups during class reading time. Offering children choice regarding texts to read aloud also helps make the experience more learner-led. For instance, teachers can suggest a shortlist of five empathy-focused novels and offer a book pitch about each before the class vote some days later. In a younger class, children can be invited to place counters in the pot next to the picture book they wish to hear that day. Equally, schools run 'You Choose Fridays' when children select which teacher's read-aloud session (variously focused on poetry, scary stories, books about animals, etc.) they would like to attend. RfP is an act of volition not imposition, so, in addition, in independent reading time children need to be able to choose what text they want to read.

Activity

Watch the video of classroom practice entitled Supporting Independent Reading Time:

https://www.researchrichpedagogies.org/research/theme/independent-reading

In this, you can see how a class of Year 6 Bristol children participate in reading time and how their teacher, Becky Barnard (née Thomson), ensures this time is *their* reading time.

As you watch make a note of:

- Becky's rationale for this time;
- the children's engagement;
- the range of activities in which they are engaged;
- the social support for reading offered in this time.

Consider the implications for making reading time in your class more LIST. What aspects do you want to develop?

Case study

Ben Harris, from Dunmow St Mary's Primary School in Essex, worked across an academic year to improve the quality of his reading aloud provision. He was not worried about his ability to bring a story to life, nor about his reading repertoire; he was confident that he knew some excellent texts that he could share with his Year 6 children. What concerned Ben was that in a reading attitude survey he undertook with his class (from the OU website), he found some children didn't really like the genres he was choosing for reading aloud time and as a result were less than keen to chat about the book.

So, he planned to develop the children's enjoyment of being read to regularly and to enrich the quality of their responses through informal book talk. Ben held a class meeting to review the

→

choices of book they might read together and explained that he had noticed many had begun to enjoy 'real-life' fictional genres. He shared four possible read-alouds (*Jelly* (Jo Cotterill), *Front Desk* (Kelly Yang), *The Boy at the Back of the Classroom* (Onjali Q. Rauf) and *Pax* (Sara Pennypacker)). The class chose *Jelly*, and Ben sought to avoid his normal pattern of regularly checking they understood key vocabulary and were following. Instead, he worked to give them 'the big-picture' and allowed the motivating power of the text to work its magic and draw them in.

To trigger book talk, Ben used Chambers' (2011) *Tell Me* structure which includes attention to what children like and dislike and what puzzles and patterns they notice. This worked well, especially when one child created her own 'story-time grid', based on these headers, to record her thinking as she listened. Several children also took up this idea, though it was not compulsory, and the resultant discussions were richer than he had previously heard in his class. Their discussions often spilled over into reading time and Ben noticed children began to seek out other books by Jo Cotterill, which indicated that reading aloud and informal book talk were impacting on their wider reading choices.

As Ben found, a relaxed interactive RfP pedagogy is key to the development of engaged young readers. Like Becky in the video noted above, Ben actively sought to avoid leading the children, and imposing his version of pleasure upon them. He gave them considerable agency as young readers, while still offering passionate and informed support. He also made time to talk informally about their 'books in common' that were read aloud and came to recognise such conversational talk as a key marker of his emerging community of readers.

Reading Teachers as members of the community

Developing children's desire to read is challenging. We cannot demand they find pleasure in texts, but we can entice and engage them as readers, and create relaxed invitational spaces in which book talk is valued. If we are also involved as fellow readers in these spaces, then we are arguably better positioned to support the young to develop positive reader identities. In one sense, all teachers are readers: many choose to read in order to imagine, to satisfy their curiosity and immerse themselves in print or online. Others find it hard to make the time for such reading, having slipped out of the habit or having never found texts that offer them a line of pleasurable readings and past satisfactions as readers. Some though, whom I denote with a capital R and capital T, develop as Reading Teachers (RTs). They do much more than share their enthusiasm for reading; they hold up a mirror to their own practices as readers and consider the possible classroom consequences in order to support child readers. RTs are socially interactive reading role models who eagerly take part in conversations with children about reading and work to help the young make their own choices and share their views and preferences. RTs play a key role in building reciprocal and interactive reading communities in their own classrooms and across the school.

Research focus

Research reveals that RTs are highly reflective professionals who make a positive difference to children's identities as readers and their pleasure in reading (Cremin et al., 2014). They create rich and productive relationships with the young based on their wider understanding of reading as social, affective and relational (Cremin, 2019b). As fellow readers, they share their own reading histories and experiences, invite the children to share theirs, and respect both diversity and difference. As children become aware that their RTs are genuinely readers themselves and interested in their own reading practices and personal responses, reading becomes a more shared, sociable experience in school. This has consequences for reading at home.

Activity

Watch this video of Jon Biddle and I being interviewed about what characterises reading communities and ways to build them in the classroom, as well as across the school and beyond. Jon is the English leader from Moorlands Primary Academy (Great Yarmouth):

https://researchrichpedagogies.org/research/theme/reading-communities

Make a note of:

- the principles I outline based on the TaRs research;
- the strategies that Jon describes to involve parents in the reading community;
- the online and digital spaces that Jon uses;
- the ways Jon helps children explore their own and their families' reading histories.

Consider what strategies you might use to help build engaged communities of readers in your class.

Case study

Jon Biddle, aware he values the supportive discussion he has with colleagues, tried as a Reading Teacher to build such opportunities in school and worked to develop more equivalent reading relationships between staff, children and family members. The staff sought to offer additional support to their most vulnerable children, several of whom were not keen readers. Jon therefore set up, among many other initiatives, a reading buddy system which involved staff members (including the caretaker and administrators) volunteering to buddy with a child.

→

These pairs met weekly in lunchtimes or other liminal spaces in the day to chat about what they were reading, and to read to and with each other. Some children brought in a favourite book from home to read, some recommended books to their adult buddy and gradually new relationships around reading were built. Another benefit was a marked increase in book talk around the school, with staff asking for recommendations from each other for their buddies.

In addition, Jon led a #MyDadreads Twitter campaign, which involved inviting children's fathers to Tweet a picture of themselves caught reading. This proved popular with over 40 dads involved and children proudly sharing and retweeting their dad's photos. Later #MyMumreads was offered and when the school ran #OurCommunityReads, 101-year-old Doris, a local resident, had her picture tweeted while reading! Jon also ran another mini project to stretch out to the community, entitled Poetry Post. Each term, he invited his class to share their love of poetry with the local community by writing out a poem of their own (or by a favourite poet) and then delivering them around the village. They also visited a care home to read some poetry and received several letters, tweets and emails from community members, some of whom also sent back copies of their own favourite poems. In these ways, Jon sought to connect his class, the school and the wider community through reading and showed the children that adults also enjoy reading.

Learning outcomes review

Now that you have read this chapter, you should understand:

- why it is important to build a community of engaged readers;
- the key features of such reading for pleasure communities;
- why teachers' knowledge of texts and RfP pedagogy is central;
- how you can build a community of children who love reading.

Conclusion

To build communities of engaged readers, teachers need to take a broadly social view of being a reader and offer appropriate support based on their own knowledge of texts, of their children and a planned pedagogy that nurtures reader agency and children's ownership of their own RfP. In these communities, new spaces for children and teachers to participate in shared talk about reading, to hear stories and to read alone and with others serve to kindle their interest, excitement and pleasure in being readers. Enjoyment in reading will be central to the culture and ethos of the classroom and will be sustained by interactive and reciprocal reader relationships. Such communities are energy intensive but are well worth the time and effort involved. The will to read influences the skill, and vice versa (OECD, 2002), and being a reader in childhood not only influences children's later academic achievements, it also supports their social and emotional well-being. Reading communities nurture a love of reading.

References

Centre for Literacy in Primary Education (CLPE) (2019) *Reflecting Realities: Survey of Ethnic Representation within UK Children's Literature 2018*. London: CLPE.

Chambers, A. (2011) *Tell Me: Children, Reading and Talk*. Stroud: Thimble Press.

Clark, C. and Teravainen, A. (2017) *What it Means to be a Reader at Age 11*. London: National Literacy Trust.

Cremin, T., Mottram, M., Powell, S., Collins, R. and Safford, K. (2014) *Building Communities of Engaged Readers: Reading for Pleasure*. London and NY: Routledge.

Cremin, T. (2019a) *Teachers' Knowledge of Children's Literature: The Cornerstone of Reading for Pleasure*. Scottish Book Trust and the First Minister's Reading Challenge. Available at: https://www.readingchallenge.scot/blog/2019-03/teachers-knowledge-childrens-literature-cornerstone-reading-pleasure

Cremin, T. (2019b) Teachers as readers and writers, in V. Bowers (ed.), *Debates in Primary Education*. London: Routledge.

Cremin, T. and Durning. A. (2020) Developing reading for pleasure across the school: research and practice, in L. Rolls and M. Green (eds), *Unlocking Research: Intellectualising Professional Development in Primary Education*. London: Routledge.

Cremin, T., Bearne, E., Mottram, M. and Goodwin, P. (2008) Exploring teachers' knowledge of children's literature. *Cambridge Journal of Education*, 38 (4): 449–64.

Department for Education (2011) *Teachers' Standards*. Available at: https://www.gov.uk/government/publications/teachers-standards (accessed 19 December 2018).

Department for Education (DfE) (2013) *The National Curriculum in England: Key Stages 1 and 2 Framework Document*. Available at: https://www.gov.uk/government/publications/national-curriculum-in-england-primary-curriculum (accessed 30 April 2020).

Department for Education (2018) *Schools, Pupils and their Characteristics: January 2018*. London: DfE.

Kalb, G. and van Ours, J.C. (2013) Reading to young children: a head-start in life? *Melbourne Institute of Applied Economic and Social Research* Working Paper No. 17/13. Available at SSRN: http://ssrn.com/abstract=2267171 or http://dx.doi.org/10.2139/ssrn.2267171

Kucirkova, N. and Cremin, T. (2020) *Reading for Pleasure in the Digital Age: Mapping Reader Engagement*. London: SAGE.

Merga, K.M. and Ledger, S. (2018) Parents' views on reading aloud to their children: beyond the early years. *Australian Journal of language and Literacy*, 41(3): 177–89.

Moses, L. and Kelly, L. (2018) 'We're a little loud. That's because we like to read!': developing positive views of reading in a diverse, urban first grade. *Journal of Early Childhood Literacy*, 18(3): 307–37.

National Union of Teachers (NUT) (2016) *Getting Everyone Reading for Pleasure*. London: NUT.

OECD (2002) *Reading for Change: Results from PISA 2000*. Available at: www.pisa.oecd.org (accessed 21 August 2020).

Ofsted (2019) Reading in the Education Inspection Framework. Sarah Hubbard keynote at Brighter Futures for Our Children conference, 13 January. Reading.

Open University (n.d.) Reading for pleasure website. (This practical site offers teacher support as they develop communities of readers. It includes reviews, practical classroom strategies, research summaries and over 400 examples of teachers' practice informed by the research.) Available at: https://ourfp.org/ (accessed 21 August 2020).

Sullivan, A. and Brown, M. (2015) Reading for pleasure and progress in vocabulary and mathematics. *British Educational Research Journal*, 41(6): 971–91.

Walker, J. (2017) *Are we Dahl Dependent?* Available at: https://jonnywalkerteaching. wordpress.com/2017/03/25/dahl-dependency-break-the-cycle/ (accessed 21 August 2020).

2 Supporting Children to Enjoy Reading in EYFS and KS1

Cathy Lawson, Megan Stephenson and Samantha Wilkes

Learning outcomes

By reading this chapter you will have considered:

- how to establish a high-quality reading environment for all EYFS and KS1 pupils;
- how to combine the teaching of discrete phonics with the use of high-quality whole books;
- how, through developing independence in young readers, a love of reading can be established;
- how all the above contribute to promote a lifelong love of reading.

Development Matters (2017)

This chapter relates to the following areas of the Statutory Framework

The EYFS framework Development Matters (DfE, 2017) puts reading within the specific areas of learning, within Literacy.

The importance of the Prime Area – Communication and Language – is broken down into three strands:

- *Listening and attention – Early Learning Goal* Children listen attentively in a range of situations. They listen to stories, accurately anticipating key events and respond to what they hear with relevant comments, questions or actions. They give their attention to what others say and respond appropriately, while engaged in another activity.
- *Understanding – Early Learning Goal* Children follow instructions involving several ideas or actions. They answer 'how' and 'why' questions about their experiences and in response to stories or events.

- *Speaking – Early Learning Goal* Children express themselves effectively, showing awareness of listeners' needs. They use past, present and future forms accurately when talking about events that have happened or are to happen in the future. They develop their own narratives and explanations by connecting ideas or events.

(DfE, 2017, pp16–29)

Teachers' Standards

1. Set high expectations which inspire, motivate and challenge pupils:

- establish a safe and stimulating environment for pupils, rooted in mutual respect;
- set goals that stretch and challenge pupils of all backgrounds, abilities and dispositions.

2. Promote good progress and outcomes for pupils:

- demonstrate knowledge and understanding of how pupils learn and how this impacts on teaching.

3. Demonstrate good subject and curriculum knowledge:

- have a secure knowledge of the relevant subject(s) and curriculum areas, foster and maintain pupils' interest in the subject, and address misunderstandings;
- demonstrate an understanding of and take responsibility for promoting high standards of literacy, articulacy and the correct use of standard English, whatever the teacher's specialist subject.

Curriculum links

Pupils' reading and rereading of books that are closely matched to their developing phonic knowledge and knowledge of common exception words supports their fluency, as well as increasing their confidence in their reading skills. Fluent word reading greatly assists comprehension, especially when pupils come to read longer books (DfE, 2013, p11).

Pupils should have extensive experience of listening to, sharing and discussing a wide range of high-quality books with the teacher, other adults and each other to engender a love of reading at the same time as they are reading independently (DfE, 2013, p12).

Introduction

In this chapter we explore how the high demands of a curriculum-heavy content can be met through the creative planning, teaching and delivery of engaging material. This chapter draws on the previous research explored by Cremin (see Chapter 1) and demonstrates how reading cultures can be established from the earliest days in Foundation Stage and throughout KS1. We consider how instructional teaching of systematic synthetic phonics (SSP) can be expertly balanced with the introduction of high-quality texts that engage children and help develop a culture of and a thirst for reading. Excellent teaching practices will be explored to demonstrate how the scaffolding of young children's learning enables them to become competent independent readers. Moreover, these young readers are further supported through embedding of such cultures school-wide. The benefits gained from delivering such pedagogy in turn encourages pupils to share their newfound knowledge and confidence with their peers, school and family communities. Expanding imaginations and working hand in hand to promote developing, competent readers is the key. Emphasis is placed on introducing the youngest readers to a culture of reading from within their environmental experiences and everyday lives. This develops as pupils learn the key skills they need to explore longer and wider varieties of materials. Whole-school approaches are identified, and exemplary practice reviewed to support readers with developing their own methods, which in turn scaffold and support the children in their care towards a lifelong love of reading.

Early and pre-reading experiences – setting the scene

When we consider key aspects of our childhood, what are the features that come to mind? Often it is a teacher, a story, a holiday and more … The experience of being read to in our formative years is one that can have lifelong positive effects. Bottrill (2018) writes passionately about these early, embedded behaviours around books, story-writing and reading habits and the key role that practitioners play in these experiences. Much consideration is paid to the secure underpinning of speaking and listening in Early Years and the wealth of opportunities for these to take place in engaging and child-led ways. Essential to this is the vibrant and imaginative planning and delivery of the curriculum.

The importance of stories and high-quality storytelling to teachers and children alike is supported by the work of Medwell *et al.* (2017). They discuss the element of everyone being a storyteller and that this supports a child's way of making sense of the world around them. This, in turn, links to creating and thinking critically. Figure 2.1 offers ideas of how children can demonstrate their creativity and thinking.

Think of the escapism, the endless possibilities, the awe and wonder of imagining you are someone else, somewhere else and creating your own beginning, middle and end to your narrative. What would be your story setting, the characters you create and the adventures they embark upon? The 'journey through to other worlds, to take on other roles and to learn, breaking down barriers in the process' (Cremin *et al.*, 2015, p101). Cremin *et al.* consider this the window to imaginatively exploring fiction.

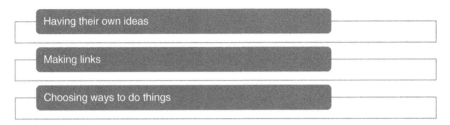

Figure 2.1   Highlights the strands of creating and thinking critically (British Association for Early Childhood Education, 2012, p5)

Rich storytelling and high-quality book immersive environments come in many different forms and attract children in a variety of unique ways. They are vital places and spaces however they are constructed, to draw children into the world of fiction. It is key that practitioners charged with fostering that love of storytelling, imagination and escapism for children, allow themselves to become part of this carefree world and embrace the endless possibilities of what stories can and should be. Bottrill (2018) asks the question: 'What should reading be?' and suggests:

- joyful
- nurturing
- warm
- purposeful
- gripping
- engaging.

Activity

Can you expand on the suggestions of Bottrill? Answer the questions in Figure 2.2 overleaf to allow your imagination to flow.

To add to this, our thoughts may turn to further adjectives and emotional experiences such as: *fun, exciting, sad, scary* and *silly*. A memorable birthday party; holiday; arrival of a sibling; or a puppy to your family are everyday and familiar experiences in young children's lives that can be used in retelling or storytelling. These examples have all formed the basis for many high-quality stories building from

(Continued)

(Continued)

the known to the unknown for children and supporting them to make sense of the world.

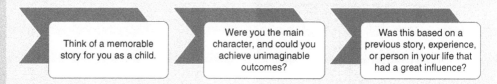

Think of a memorable story for you as a child.

Were you the main character, and could you achieve unimaginable outcomes?

Was this based on a previous story, experience, or person in your life that had a great influence?

Figure 2.2

Think about a memorable book or storytelling scenario from your childhood and consider what emotive experiences it stirred in you. List these and compare against the suggestions above.

Research focus

Gamble writes about reflecting 'on how your reading practices have contributed to your acquisition of cultural literacy and your formation of a reading identity' (2019, p17). Her research details the importance of book talk, sharing books as a family and trips to the library; all contributing to developing a positive image for us as readers. As practising teachers, it is vital that we not only make these links with our prior influences, but importantly also consider the home influences for a child, and the impact this will have on their relationship with books and reading. The formative years before nursery and school are fundamental to the stages that follow.

Creating an immersive reading environment in Early Years

How these are planned for in different settings, leads to creative licence, individuality and richness. Enabling environments are woven within the *Characteristics of Effective Learning* (DfE, 2012, p4) and this is closely linked with the approach the school takes on the balance between child-led and adult-led schema.

The following examples will help to support practitioners in developing such a culture.

Story areas: indoors and outdoors

Rooms and outdoor spaces need cosy reading areas that invite children to develop a love of stories and storytelling. Providing a variety of stories and props will motivate and support reading.

Story spoons or story stones painted as familiar characters – for example, from *The Gruffalo* by Julia Donaldson – allow characters and objects to be manipulated to help build a story. Events and characters can be imaginatively bought to life through the introduction of finger and glove puppets, materials, wooden blocks, natural resources and instruments.

Encouraging children to love stories and become well versed in the content through revisiting familiar texts, such as traditional tales, is a tried and trusted approach for teachers. While immersed in a book, children can make use of the pictures to retell the story and even read to their friends. It is important to ensure that all props and books are at the children's height, so that they can access them at all times. Here the role of the adult is key, sitting in the areas to create narratives with the children evokes the creativity and provides a positive role model.

Working in Partnership

Engaging parents at home	Stay and read	Weekend friend
Inviting parents and carers into nursery and school to create a reading den to share favourite stories, as well as reading in an unusual place while at home, e.g. under the table, in the garden, etc. Online communication tools offer the possibility of these fun photos being shared, and moving on from how we may think of reading and storytelling taking place.	Offering a 'Stay and Read' session throughout the week that allows parents to come and observe staff reading as well as playing games to help develop reading skills. Modelling the power and richness that comes from sharing a story.	A specially child-chosen weekend friend can encourage and support families to enjoy books, some they may not be familiar with, as the child takes the book and a prop/puppet from the story home. This is then returned on Monday with a talking activity to share their adventures. By adding some hot chocolate to the weekend friend goody-bag you have created a wonderful storytime resource.

Figure 2.3

Working in partnership

Sharing the importance of the immersive reading environment, threading this through the areas of learning and sharing texts together, should be closely linked, where possible, with engaging the valuable partnership of parents/carers. Building a strong relationship between home and children's early school experience supports lifelong reading patterns and behaviours in children. Having a clear and deep knowledge of child development is essential for practitioners. Through their depth of knowledge, practitioners can create the opportunities for engaging parents and carers in activities which will promote a shared understanding and value of storytelling.

Figure 2.3 demonstrates how schools can 'work in partnership' with their communities.

By the time children are three years old their developing language skills, experience of positive relationships and a growing love of words and reading are all fully underway and impacting on their lives (Bottrill, 2018, p124).

The case study below demonstrates creative practice within an Early Years setting and gives an example of how an Early Years practitioner ignites the imagination in young children, supporting them in becoming young storytellers.

Case study: developing story language in Early Years

A highly experienced Early Years teacher, within a large primary school in south Leeds, plans for a variety of high-quality books, reading and storytelling to be at the heart of both indoor and outdoor provision. She observes the children and plans in the moment to continuously enhance their opportunities to listen, focus, react and begin to verbalise their interest and engagement in the 'reading world'. The children are immersed in worlds of characters, acting out through a technique known as 'helicopter stories'. This is the technique of storytelling and story-acting based on the work by the American author Viviane Gussin Paley, but introduced to the UK by Trisha Lee. The teacher describes how the opportunity arose to take part in a 'story scribing' session and she enthuses, 'It was magical and has led to each half term every child in my class wanting to create a story.'

The teacher explains, 'The child thinks of story and I write it down, word for word. I show them an A5 piece of paper, and it can be a short story or page after page. The child's story can be one word or enough to fill the paper; everything is celebrated. Through encouraging the child to use story language I let them make up a story. They love it when we create a rectangular story stage with masking tape, either indoors or out. This instantly allows the children to believe they have a stage and cannot wait to perform inside it, while their friends sit around the outside.

The child who has created the story stands in the story stage and then I read their story. They become one of their characters or objects. Friends are also invited to join in. Suddenly, their words become a magical story for them and their friends to perform. The story scribes are displayed and often children ask to return to these and act them out again and again. Children who are able to have written stories for their friends.'

The above case study demonstrates that, at such a young age, all children can become storytellers and authors.

Activity

Make a list of the links this form of oral storytelling has with early reading.

This section has identified how early introductions to stories and high-quality texts promotes connections and relationships with words and language. This is a time to develop children's talk, play and wider curriculum experiences. A 'language-rich' environment should prioritise *talking with* children. Evoking children's connections and familiarity with high-quality texts and the experience of stories, both with words and also through picture books, promotes a growing love of playing with language and the endless possibilities of storytelling.

Emphasis has been placed on introducing the youngest readers to a culture of reading within their local environment and everyday lives. Abundant language and book-rich environments help create the memories and the planned-for teaching and learning opportunities that arise from these.

The importance of teaching phonics

As children begin to expand their knowledge and experience of 'reading' through engaging in a variety of activities, we can begin to appreciate that, as well as enjoying sharing books with others, they will start to make links between the marks on a page and spoken language. Such 'early concepts about print' (Elborn, 2016, p37) should be developed and encouraged before more formal teaching of phonics begins. Crucial here is that we encourage children to also listen out for and use auditory discrimination in order to begin to recognise sounds within words (Elborn, 2016).

Figure 2.4 identifies *crucial concepts* children should experience prior to the teaching of reading through phonics.

Know some terminology about books, e.g. title, picture, word, letter
Hold a book the correct way up
Turn the pages one at a time from front to back
Understand that print, in English, goes from left to right and from the top of the page to the bottom
Understand that the words (print) carry meaning rather than the picture
Recognise a few words
Begin to point to words when they are spoken

Figure 2.4   Concepts about print (Elborn, 2016, pp37–9)

The idea that spoken language and the knowledge of written words can be developed simultaneously was advocated by Rose (DfES, 2006) and can be represented in the 'simple view of reading' (see Figure 2.5).

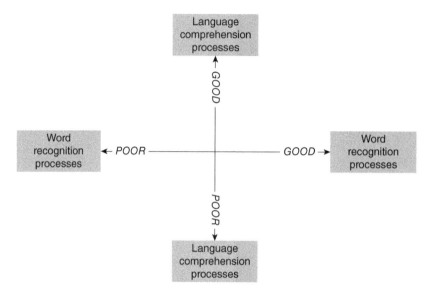

Figure 2.5   The simple view of reading (Gough and Tunmer, 1986)

This was further developed by Scarborough (2001) when she introduced the 'reading rope' as a more detailed representation, identifying the complexities of how children learn to *process* the language they are being introduced to in order to learn to read fluently.

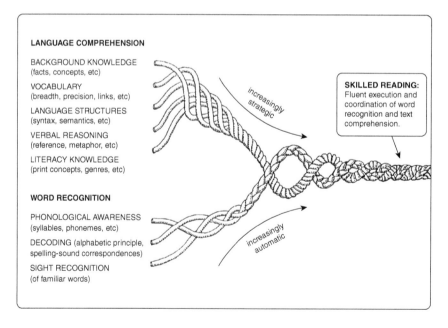

Figure 2.6   The many strands that are woven into skilled reading

(Scarborough, 2001, p25)

Figure 2.6 demonstrates the complexities of how decoding and comprehension work together to encourage fluency in reading.

Rose (DfES, 2006) recommended that children use phonics as the 'prime approach in learning to decode (to read) and encode (to write/spell) print' (DfES, 2006, p70).

Teaching discrete systematic synthetic phonics while developing a love of reading

We have demonstrated that children, as early readers, begin to develop their language comprehension and are also beginning to acquire some phonological awareness. They then go on to embed their phonemic knowledge through more formal teaching, as they progress through EYFS (Jolliffe and Waugh, 2018, p13).

It is recommended that the children are taught phonics in a systematic and structured way (DfES, 2006; Johnston and Watson, 2014; Waugh *et al.*, 2015). To aid this instruction, the government document *Letters and Sounds* (2007) outlines how teachers should teach phonics. It subdivides the teaching of phonics into six phases and incorporates a suggested lesson structure for a daily phonics lessons:

> **Phase 1** of *Letters and Sounds*, addresses the need for younger children to develop their awareness of spoken sounds which is detailed earlier in this chapter.
>
> **Phase 2:** Teaches at least 19 letters and moves children on from oral blending and segmentation to blending and segmenting with letters.
>
> **Phase 3**: Teaches another 25 graphemes, most of them comprising two letters (digraph), so the children can represent each of about 42 phonemes by a grapheme.
>
> **Phase 4:** Consolidates children's knowledge of graphemes in reading and spelling words containing adjacent consonants and polysyllabic words.
>
> **Phase 5**: Allows children to broaden their knowledge of graphemes and phonemes for use in reading and spelling. Children learn new graphemes and alternative pronunciations for these and graphemes they already know, where relevant.
>
> **Phase 6**: Children become fluent readers and increasingly accurate spellers.
>
> (DfES, 2007)

Since the publication of *Letters and Sounds,* many additional schemes have been produced that emulate this style and structure. All advocate the decoding of individual sounds as the first step towards early reading.

Educators need to plan and teach phonics using a range of creative approaches in order to maintain children's interest and encourage their progression. Some examples of different teaching strategies are outlined in the case study below.

Case study: teaching discrete phonics creatively

Wendy is an experienced Year 1 teacher in West Yorkshire. She teaches phonics discretely to her class every day for 30 minutes. She begins each lesson by reviewing previously taught phonemes and common exception words. She does this in a variety of ways, e.g. using flash-cards, asking children to blend spoken phonemes and write the graphemes and words on individual whiteboards, 'speed read' games and 'phoneme spotter' texts. She does this as she noticed that if she used the same teaching strategy every day, the children would 'remem-ber' what to say and she couldn't assess the pupils' understanding very effectively. She then introduces the new learning, usually using the IWB. Wendy has found that most of the children are engaged for a short period of time during this part of the lesson. Wendy is then keen for pupils to practise putting the new learning into context and includes a variety of practi-cal activities for the children during the phonics lesson. For example, when the children are learning about the alternative graphemes for the phoneme /ai/ they have a role-play picnic and eat *grapes* and *raisins* while wearing *capes* and 'sheltering from' the *rain*. Children also engage in and freely access phonics games and mark-making opportunities. Wendy displays the key words around the classroom and takes opportunities to assess the children's reading and spelling skills using the new graphemes.

The case study demonstrates how, although Wendy teaches phonics daily in a discrete format, she then immerses the pupils with further experiences of using the sounds and words they are reading within the whole learning environment. The children's phonic knowledge is then formatively assessed to allow for effective progression. The children's phonic knowledge is also assessed more formally in the phonic screening check (PSC) at the end of Year 1, where children are asked to decode a mixture of real and pseudo words.

Teaching phonics through real reading

It is important to remember that reading text is not simply about decoding the letters but includes all the strands highlighted in the 'reading rope' above. If we consider that the purpose of reading is enjoyment, and to gain information, it is easy to understand that children's phonological skills need to be put into context by applying them to the reading and enjoyment of texts. In fact, a key recommendation of Rose was that: 'Phonic work should be set within a broad and rich language curriculum' (DfES, 2006, p70). As well as teaching phonics discretely, teachers should link phonics to high-quality texts, storytelling and real reading to maintain children's engagement and developing a love of books.

Activity

Read the text *The Way Back Home* by Oliver Jeffers. Suppose that you are using the text with the children in your class. You intend to use the text to teach them an aspect of Phase 3 phonics, e.g. practising CVC blending and segmenting and learning new digraphs.

How could you teach aspects of Phase 3 phonics when you are reading the text?

Consider: what activities and resources, linked to the text, would be needed in your classroom in order to develop children's word recognition skills and children's language comprehension skills?

Research focus

Following her study, Carter (2019) expressed some concern that teaching children phonics using the strategy outlined in *Letters and Sounds* (DfES, 2007), in preparation for the Phonics Screening Check (PSC), caused some children to believe that learning phonics was a separate skill to learning how to read. Davis shares her concerns regarding the PSC and argues that sometimes it's only when you've worked out the context that you know how to say a word (Davis, 2014).

Mantei and Kervin (2019) go further and suggest that teaching phonics according to a specific programme contradicts a teacher's desire to teach children according to their learning needs and interests, as advocated by established pedagogies. They argue that, by assessing children's reading using running records, teaching phonics using carefully selected resources and in modelled, guided and independent reading lessons, teachers can still teach phonics systematically. They say that:

> If we accept that language is a living and evolving entity, we need contemporary literacy pedagogies that have real world application. That means we need to teach reading and writing using real and complex texts embedded in real and complex contexts that can support learners to make meaning.

> (Mantei and Kervin, 2019, p14)

They continue:

> Teaching phonics in context reflects the pedagogies of contemporary classrooms. It is systematic and personalised to the needs, interests and abilities of each child. Also, it sets them up to engage with the increasingly complex and sophisticated texts that they must deal with throughout and beyond primary school.

> (Mantei and Kervin, 2019, p14)

The debate continues to rumble on; however, what is evident is that children learn best when using a variety and combination of teaching strategies.

Harnessing and encouraging a love of reading and real reading

Once children have mastered the mechanical skills of decoding short singular lines of text in books, they should be gradually encouraged to read more challenging material with growing independence and fluency. Developing comprehension skills as they go is essential, so children begin to make connections between common aspects of reading. These behaviours not only support further understanding of text content, but also encourage the beginnings of real independent reading of longer, whole books of choice. For the purpose of this chapter we will call these children our developing readers (DRs).

Dombey (2010) emphasised how a balanced approach to the teaching of decoding and comprehension was so important for beginning and developing readers. As well as learning the mechanics of reading, children must be encouraged and supported to focus on making sense of the text. This means 'ensuring that classrooms are filled with interesting written texts – on screens as well as on paper – and that children are given rich experiences of putting these texts to use' (2010, p5).The English National Curriculum (DfE, 2013) expresses the importance of children being exposed to a range of spoken language and a wide variety of book genres in order to develop pleasure in reading: poems, stories and non-fiction, along with exposure to multimodal digital sources, should all be used to develop an immersive culture of reading. Perkins (2016) writes, 'Whatever the nature of a text, what we are reading matters and it is through encounters with texts that children learn what it is to be a reader' (2016, p10).

Children encouraged to do this begin to look out for texts they enjoy and therefore often want to read more for themselves; it is essential at this point that such enthusiasm is harnessed and developed further. 'Teachers as readers' is a well-researched area (see Chapter 1 for details). Cremin notes that being a Reading Teacher is essential if this way of working is to be promoted. In the final part of this chapter we will focus on the details of how such can be established and developed throughout KS1.

Modelling to children and portraying ourselves as readers is key to supporting DRs in order to demonstrate 'good' reading, advance skills and build confidence. Encouraging children to see the value in reading and maintaining a thirst for accessing a range of texts and disciplines is essential. Children need to see themselves reflected in the texts they read in order to support their growing understanding and identity. Therefore, teachers should continue to review and recommend established authors, but also the work of current, new vibrant writers. It is always important that, as educators, we establish a basis for inclusive and diverse texts. For more information and recommended texts, see Chapter 7, in this book, on inclusive and diverse texts.

Reading aloud to and with children: sharing the love for books

Many educators and book lovers welcomed the increased emphasis in the 2014 National Curriculum of reading aloud to children. Demonstrations of reading out loud for pleasure in classrooms had appeared to ebb away under previous government strategies, with part books and 'extracts' from texts being favoured. Jolliffe and Waugh also argued that a thirst for knowledge and an interest in children's literature had been revived more recently through the reading of whole texts and that, by 'reading to children teachers demonstrate that they value reading themselves' (2018, p57). They also noted other benefits when allocating set times to this practice, including an increase in pupil's positive well-being and most notably a sense of 'togetherness' and social cohesion that sharing a class book can promote. Being a Reading Teacher is crucial here. Cremin (2019) concluded that teachers needed to have a wider range of knowledge of children's literature in order to develop and establish excellent reading for pleasure (RfP) pedagogy and ethos within the classroom.

Research focus

Gamble (2019) encouraged groups of teachers and students to list why being a reader is important. She noted how, for many, the benefits of developing an improved reading style through the practice of reading aloud was also complemented by the additional advantage of pupils reporting improvements in well-being and community. She states:

> Reading in a social context allows us to share our thoughts with others. Then we can discuss what we have read or heard read and as a result we react and interact with others. Subsequently, 'we learn to negotiate and develop a better understanding firstly of ourselves and then of others'.

> (2019, p291)

When teachers model reading aloud to their pupils, they are demonstrating key skills necessary for our young readers to develop. Most notably the *intonation* and *expression* needed to maintain a listener's interest. The following case study demonstrates how, by reading aloud to pupils the teacher supports the children in suspending their disbelief and encourages them to focus in on developing and understanding of characterisation and plot.

Case study : modelling reading aloud to pupils

Matthew is a Year 1 teacher in a school in Bradford. He plans into all his English units of work the opportunity to read aloud to the pupils. He encourages his pupils to devise voices and actions for how certain characters in the books should sound and move. Asking the pupils to listen to the dialogue read using slightly differing tones, he then allows children to choose 'how this character will sound' throughout the book. Matthew explains that previously, when training to teach, he would watch his teacher sit down and read to the children. However, at times the teacher 'forgot' how a character sounded, causing, at first, amusement, but sometimes consternation from the pupils.

→

'I decided then and there that I would make my reading to pupils a focal point in the classroom,' he says. 'By giving the pupils ownership of what the character sounds like and the gestures they use I am encouraging them to play a part in developing characterisation and providing opportunities for them to demonstrate their understanding of the character. This is turn supports their evaluation of how and why certain aspects of the story unfold.'

Planning using the above techniques Matthew is working with his pupils, providing clues for the listener to draw upon and in turn promoting an understanding of the narrative through immersive practice. When listening to their teacher read the children do not have to focus on the mechanics of reading individually and therefore can process the language as it is read to them. This supports their understanding and comprehension. It also gives the children the opportunity to discuss the actions of characters and develop their own thoughts on the text.

Research focus

A research project conducted in a London borough by Duncan (2015) identified several gains reported from reading aloud. These included an increase in memorising texts, understanding the materials and reviewing the content of what had been read collectively. Bearne and Reedy (2018) discuss further the opportunities reading aloud with pupils can provide and the value of reading longer texts to children. Providing access to materials beyond a child's level of fluency (at an instructional level) provides them with more access to other texts and the chance to process complex materials – imagining the real and imagined worlds on offer. Moreover, as educators we are also allowing developing readers to *listen* and *respond* without having to demonstrate the conventions of processing the language as a reader; children are, as such, able to process the information as a *listener*. And for many pupils this provides an easier platform to explore and begin to empathise with characters' feelings and predicaments. As Cremin explores in Chapter 1 of this book, it is essential that children both hear others (including their teachers and also their peers) reading aloud, in order to gain the most from the experience, and begin to foster the learning and reading for pleasure (RfP) pedagogy.

Activity

Choose an age appropriate, recommended high-quality text from your school library:

- plan a section to read aloud to a group of children;
- practise using a range of voices;
- read the text to the pupils;
- ask them to choose their favourite character's voice.

What are the values and pitfalls of encouraging pupils to read aloud to their peers?

In what way can we prepare, encourage and support pupils to read aloud in class and at home?

Promoting independence in developing readers

In order to support developing readers to become more independent from a young age, all agencies need to tap into children's interests and motivations. Fletcher *et al.* (2012) conducted a study looking at the key factors involved in this early motivation. They concluded the following to be vital motivators:

- reading aloud to pupils;

- promoting books of interest to pupils;

- pupils recommending books to one another;

- reading and talking individually with pupils to discuss what they enjoyed and why these books were preferred.

Cremin (2010) writes about the need to carefully balance the continued teaching of reading instruction with that of reading for pleasure. She writes about extending pupils' opportunities to, 'hear, read, inhabit, explore and respond to potent text' (2010, p2) Many authors, including Janan and Wray (2012), emphasise the need for teachers to use their professional knowledge and judgement when choosing texts to use in reading lessons. They discuss the need for readability and accessibility. Personalising the learning materials and planning for specific groups of children is key here. Children need not only to be motivated by the content, but also willing to engage in what is going on.

The work of Teravainen and Clark (2017) identifies how the needs of individuals should always remain the key focus for schools when planning to develop children's independence in reading. Planning from a full range of high-quality texts and for a variety of interests, Stephenson (in Bushnell *et al.*, 2020) highlights the importance of engaging pupils through the use of 'hooks' when introducing texts to developing readers. Choosing texts that have challenging language for pupils to explore is essential, as it provides opportunities for children to extend their vocabulary. This vocabulary should be used freely in the classroom and is then often a driver for children to use in their own writing as a result.

Introducing pupils to new language and experiences through texts provides opportunities for educators to invite responses. This is called a 'reader response' approach, where teachers demonstrate their excellent subject knowledge and ability to tap into the learning using a variety of strategies (Gamble, 2019, p321).

Table 2.1 shows examples how 'reader response' can be planned to develop engaging and creative activities and promote independence and comprehension.

Table 2.1 Examples of how to encourage 'reader response' from pupils

Activity	Reader response
hook	
Teacher provides an exciting stimulus to introduce the text	Pupils explore the clues provided about the text and predict content
Question time and/or hot-seating	Children pose as *chief questioners* and formulate questions about the *characters* and *setting* as the book is read
	Teacher or other children pose as characters and attempt to answer the questions
Discussions around predicting plots/character responses	Children predict outcomes or *possible scenarios* for characters to encounter
	Record these and *return* and *review* them as the story unfolds
Recording visual responses to books	Record own *visual responses* of what is happening in text
	Use *story mapping* or *annotate individual illustrations* to demonstrate key aspects of the story
Thought bubbles of how characters are feeling and what they are thinking	Pupils record these as the book continues to reflect on *characters' experiences*, demonstrating insight into characters' thoughts and feelings
Vocabulary exploration	Record key vocabulary from texts to explore, investigate definitions and clarify understanding

'Texts need to be rich enough for rereading and have the potential for exploring layers of meaning – reading deeply' (Gamble, 2019, p321).

A deep exploration of the spoken word is central to developing the children's own use of language when exploring meaning in the texts, offering opportunities to search and pursue language to aid comprehension and maintain engagement. Each text chosen should provide a challenge but be accessible for individuals to read. The use of high-quality texts is now becoming an established form of best practice. Authors extol the virtues of planning using this format. Such a way of working is coined by some as a 'Take One Book' approach, whereby one high-quality text us used as a central tool (Stephenson, 2020, p41, cited in Bushnell *et al.*, 2020).

Lucy (a PGCE primary student at Leeds Trinity University) noted the change she saw in her pupils during her final block of school-based training when using Take One Book, an approach introduced during planning sessions at the university. Lucy noted:

> The children were engrossed in the story of *The Kiss that Missed* by D. Melling. Many of them began using the language in their work and illustrating their

own sections of the stories as a result. Parents commented on how 'motivating' this style of working was and what an impact it had had on the pupils' home reading attitudes.

She agreed that the materials need to be rich in language and provide opportunities to explore through rereading and revisiting.

Learning outcomes review

From reading this chapter you should now be able to:

- create and establish a quality reading environment for all EYFS and KS1 pupils;
- understand the importance of combining the teaching of discrete phonics with using high-quality whole books;
- recognise the strategies needed to develop independence in young readers so that a love of reading is established;
- feel more confident that by applying the above in school you can contribute to promoting a lifelong love of reading.

Conclusion: establishing a lifelong love of reading

In this chapter you should have reflected on how establishing a love of language and reading lays the foundation of learning from the earliest days of school. The use of carefully planned and orchestrated stimuli and experiences foster this love of language and learning and become an everyday practice in Foundation Stage. This knowledge builds when children begin to learn to read using the established methods of systematic synthetic teaching in phonics, but should be balanced by immersion in current high-quality inclusive and diverse texts, in order to establish harmony and reciprocity between decoding (instructional reading) and a depth of comprehension. Modelling reading and reading for pleasure (RfP) become deep-rooted within school communities as children develop independent reading behaviours and grow into developing readers (DRs). Encouragement to share their love of texts through the modelling of reading from Reading Teachers, the establishment of meaningful and whole-school approaches to celebrating reading for pleasure (RfP), and an invitation to the wider community to contribute and share their ideas. All of these become the drivers and motivators for establishing a lifelong love of reading.

References

Bearne, E. and Reedy, D. (eds) (2018) *Teaching Primary English: Subject Knowledge and Classroom Practice*. London: Routledge.

Bottrill, G. (2018) *Can I Go and Play Now?* London: SAGE.

British Association for Early Childhood Education (2012) *Development Matters in the Early Years Foundation Stage (EYFS)*. London: British Association for Early Childhood Education. Available at: https://www.foundationyears.org.uk/files/2012/03/Development-Matters-FINAL-PRINT-AMENDED.pdf (accessed 21 August 2020).

Bushnell, A. Gill, A. and Waugh, D. (2020) *Mastering Writing at Greater Depth*. London: SAGE.

Carter, J. (2019) Listening to the voices of children: an illuminative evaluation of the teaching of early reading in the light of the phonics screening check. *Literacy*, 54(1(January 2020)): 49–57.

Cremin, T. and Baker, S. (2010) Exploring teacher–writer identities in the classroom. *English Teaching: Practice and Critique*, 9(3): 8–25.

Cremin, T., Bearne, E. Mottram, M. and Goodwin, P. (2008a) Primary teachers as readers. *English in Education*, 42(1): 1–16.

Cremin, T., Bearne, E. Mottram, M. and Goodwin, P (2008b) Exploring teachers' knowledge of children's literature. *Cambridge Journal of Education*, 38(4): 449–64.

Cremin, T. (2010) Poetry teachers: Teachers who read and readers who teach poetry in Styles M., Joy L. and Whitley D. (Eds.) *Poetry and childhood*. London: Trentham, pp219–226

Cremin, T., Reedy, D., Bearne, E. and Dombey, H. (2015) *Teaching English Creatively* (2nd edn). London: Routledge.

Cremin, T. (2019) *Reading Communities: Why, What and How?* Sheffield: NATE

Davis, A. (2014) Reading lessons: why synthetic phonics doesn't work. *Guardian* Available at: https://www.theguardian.com/teacher-network/teacher-blog/2014/mar/04/reading-lessons-phonics-world-book-day (accessed 21 August 2020).

Department for Education (DfE) (2010) Phonics teaching materials: core criteria and the self-assessment process. Available at: www.gov.uk/government/publications/national-curriculum-in-england-english-programmes-of-study/national-curriculum-in-english-programmes- of- study (accessed 21 August 2020).

Department for Education (2012) *Statutory Framework for the Early Years Foundation Stage (EYFS)*. Available at: https://www.education.gov.uk/publications/standard/AllPublications/Page1/DFE-00023-2012

Department for Education (2013) *The National Curriculum in England: Key Stages 1 and 2 Framework Document*. Available at: https://www.gov.uk/government/publications/national-curriculum-in-england-primary-curriculum (accessed 30 April 2020).

Department for Education (2014) *The National Curriculum in England: English Programmes of Study*. London: DfE.

Department for Education (2017) *Statutory Framework for the Early Years Foundation Stage*. London: DfE.

Department for Employment and Education (DfEE) (1999) *All Our Futures: Creativity, Culture and Education*. London: DfEE.

Department for Education and Skills (DfES) (2006) *The Independent Review of the Teaching of Early Reading*. Available at: https://dera.ioe.ac.uk/5551/2/report.pdf (accessed 21 August 2020).

Department for Education and Skills (2007) *Letters and Sounds: Principles and Practice of High Quality Phonics*. Available at: https://assets.publishing.service.gov.uk/government/uploads/system/uploads/attachment_data/file/190599/Letters_and_Sounds_-_DFES-00281-2007.pdf (accessed 21 August 2020).

Dombey, H. (2010) *Teaching Reading: What the Evidence Says*. Leicester: UKLA.

Donaldson, J. (1999) *The Gruffalo*. London: Macmillan.

Duncan, S. (2015) Reading aloud in Lewisham: an exploration of adult reading-aloud practices. *Literacy*, 49(2): 84–90.

Elborn, S. (2016) *Handbook of Teaching Early Reading: More than Phonics*. London: UKLA.

Fletcher, J., Grimley, M., Greenwood, J. and Parkhill, F. (2012) Motivating and improving attitudes to reading in the final years of primary schooling in five New Zealand schools. *Literacy*, 46(1): 3–16.

Gamble, N. (2019) *Exploring Children's Literature: Reading Knowledge, Understanding and Pleasure* (4th edn). London: SAGE.

Gough, P.B. and Tunmer, W.E. (1986) Decoding, reading and reading disability. *Remedial and Special Education*, 7: 6–10.

Janan, D. and Wray, D. (2012) *Readbility: the limitations of an approach through formula*. Paper presented at BERA, University of Manchester, 4–6 September.

Johnston, R. and Watson, J. (2014) *Teaching Synthetic Phonics* (2nd edn). London: SAGE.

Jolliffe, W. and Waugh, D. (2018) *Mastering Primary English*. London: Bloomsbury.

Mantei, J. and Kervin, L. (2019) What's your system? Thinking about what we mean by being 'systematic' in our teaching about letter–sound relationships in context. *Practical Literacy*, 24(2).

Medwell, J., Wray, D., Minns, H., Griffiths, V. and Coates, E. (2017) *Primary English Teaching Theory and Practice*. London: SAGE.

Perkins, M. (2016) *Observing Primary Literacy* (2nd edn). London: SAGE.

Scarborough, H.S. (2001) Connecting early language and literacy to later reading (dis)abilities: evidence, theory and practice, in S. Neuman and D. Dickinson (eds), *Handbook for Research in Early Literacy*. New York: Guildford Press, pp97–110.

Teravainen, A. and Clark, C. (2017) *School Libraries: A Literature Review of Current Provision and Evidence of Impact.* London: National Literacy Trust.

Waugh, D., Carter, J. and Desmond, C. (2015) *Lessons in Teaching Phonics in Primary Schools.* London: SAGE.

Further reading

Cremin, T., Mottram, M., Collins, F., Powell, S. and Salford, K. (2008) *Teachers as Readers: Building Communities of Engaged Readers.* 2007–8 Executive Summary. London: UKLA.

Goodall, J. and Montgomery, C. (2014) Parental involvement to parental engagement: a continuum. *Education Review*, 66(4): 399–410.

Ofsted (2012) *Moving English Forward: Action to Raise Standards in English.* London: HMSO.

3 Supporting Developing Readers to Thrive through KS2 into KS3

Rachel Rudman

Learning outcomes

By reading this chapter you will have considered:

- how children's reading can be nurtured through the use of challenging texts as they move into upper Key Stage 2;
- what approaches and activities might best be employed in order to nurture developing readers;
- how a reading culture can be preserved in the transition from primary to secondary school.

Teachers' Standards

3. Demonstrate good subject and curriculum knowledge:

- have a secure knowledge of the relevant subject(s) and curriculum areas, foster and maintain pupils' interest in the subject, and address misunderstandings;
- demonstrate a critical understanding of developments in the subject and curriculum areas, and promote the value of scholarship.

4. Plan and teach well-structured lessons:

- impart knowledge and develop understanding through effective use of lesson time;
- promote a love of learning and children's intellectual curiosity.

Curriculum link

[Pupils] should be reading widely and frequently, outside as well as in school, for pleasure and information. They should be able to read silently, with good understanding, inferring the meanings of unfamiliar words, and then discuss what they have read (DfE, 2013a, p41).

Reading at key stage 3 should be wide, varied and challenging. Pupils should be expected to read whole books, to read in depth and to read for pleasure and information (DfE, 2013b, p14).

Introduction

Key Stage 2 can be an exciting time for pupils as readers. In the first years of primary school, systematic synthetic phonics teaching will have given them the means to decode increasingly detailed and complex texts. As reading confidence grows, their repertoire of texts will continually evolve and broaden (see Chapters 1 and 2 on supporting developing readers). This developing reading fluency is essential in order to access much of the curriculum in school, thus highlighting the central place of reading within the primary classroom. Indeed, it could be argued that: 'Creating capable and keen readers is the most important job that schools can do' (UKLA, 2016, p5).

As children's reading becomes more fluent, there emerges a clearer distinction between the National Curriculum requirements of reading 'for *pleasure* and *information*' (emphasis added). At the end of Key Stage 2, pupils are assessed and externally marked through Standardised Attainment Tests (SATs). The reading test consists of one-, two- and three-mark questions about three texts which cover a range of domains. Pupils are expected to be able to: retrieve information, summarise, make inferences, predict, identify, explain and make comparisons. The preparation for this can and does form the basis for much of the direct reading input within the classroom. Alongside these reading skill requirements, the National Curriculum expects pupils to read for pleasure. This is more difficult to measure tangibly and moves beyond the scope of the Key Stage 2 reading test. Nevertheless, enjoyment in reading remains essential; to focus only on the tangible test skills runs the risk of taking 'too narrow a view of what learning to read is about, reducing reading to a set of school-related, measurable competences' (Hall, 2015, p62).

The 2019 Ofsted framework identified the critical importance of reading, seeking evidence in the school being inspected that 'a rigorous approach to the teaching of reading develops learners' confidence and enjoyment in reading' (Ofsted, 2019, p10). Underpinning this was another priority, which focused on the intent to see 'the knowledge and cultural capital they (Pupils) need to succeed in life' (Ofsted, 2019, p9). Indeed, when you meet a child who reads widely for pleasure, the confidence that this offers is immediately evident in the child's vocabulary choices, wider cultural capital and enthusiasm with which books are discussed. Barbara Bleiman suggests that one of the key reasons for teaching a novel is 'to inculcate a predisposition towards reading for pleasure in students' future lives' (Bleiman, 2020, p154). While this is not measured through any external examinations, it remains a constituent part of the curriculum and vitally important in nurturing well-rounded individuals.

The National Literacy Trust annual survey in 2019 showed the importance of independent reading. It concluded that children who read daily in their free time are more than twice as likely to read above the level expected for their age as children who don't read daily (37.6 per cent versus 14.2 per cent) (National Literacy Trust, 2019, p2). If they enjoy reading, this will have a positive impact on reading capability as pupils will be able to access more complex texts if they read regularly; also this will have a positive impact on overall attainment in school. The same report found that '53% of children and young people said they enjoy reading' (National Literacy Trust, 2019, p1). This figure clearly raises questions about how to embed reading fluency, confidence and enjoyment effectively while children are in primary school. A further challenge comes in maintaining reading engagement as children move on to secondary school, since there appears to be a decline in reading as children get older (Ofsted, 2012).

This chapter will consider how we enable children to become fluent and enthusiastic readers while at primary school, and how this reading engagement might be sustained through transition to secondary school.

Using challenging texts to support developing readers throughout upper Key Stage 2

Bringing pupils on

By Key Stage 2, there are often clear differences in levels of independence among pupils in terms of reading. Some children might become 'free readers' as early as Year 2, whereas others will continue to work with structured reading schemes and move through levelled reading programmes in order to develop fluency. It is therefore important to acknowledge the potentially wide range of reading abilities in the class, which is inevitable given the complex nature of reading.

Research focus

The Education Endowment Foundation (2017) collated research around seven evidence-based strategies which can be used to support literacy development, particularly for pupils who might be struggling.

The strategies below have direct links to reading development:

• Develop pupils' language capability to support their reading and writing

This focuses on the importance of speaking and listening in order to strengthen literacy. Pupils might discuss their ideas and share thought processes through guided discussion and questioning in order to shape thinking. Whereas it might seem safer for the teacher to be asking the questions and leading such discussion, there is an argument for pupils to be given

→

more responsibility for discussing – rather than being fed – ideas around a text. The English and Media Centre research project of 2015, It's Good to Talk, found from student question-naire responses that, when faced with a challenging text, pupils were pleased to be given the responsibility of 'having to think hard'. Accompanying video footage suggested that the pupils were 'thinking harder by talking to each other' (Bleiman, 2020, p101) rather than always being given a clear steer from the teacher.

- Support pupils to develop fluent reading capabilities

As readers become more fluent, they are then freed up in terms of cognitive capacity to engage more fully with the meanings and ideas in a text. If teachers 'model fluent reading of a text' and offer opportunities for children to engage in 'repeated reading' of texts it can then embed fluency (see Chapter 2 for examples of how best practice can be used to model reading aloud to pupils).

- Teach reading comprehension strategies through modelling and supported practice (Education Endowment Foundation, 2017, p4)

Teaching of comprehension strategies in a clearly defined way can successfully nurture confidence and engagement in less assured readers. Although the range of questions in the Key Stage 2 reading test will not measure enjoyment of reading, if the reading of a text is modelled with careful questions which gradually increase the cognitive demand, children can then become more confident in their perspective about a text. If they can recall key information, summarise, make inferences and identify key ideas, then the enthusiasm around texts is likely to increase as success in analysing the text grows. The stem questions of the Key Stage 2 reading paper can offer frames for use during classroom questioning. (Refer to Chapter 2 for further ideas on how to gather 'reader response' and developing comprehension skills.)

Texts need to be carefully chosen to allow the development of key strategies around reading. Children developing as readers need specific guidance about the range of strategies they use when approaching a text for the first time. Reciprocal reading as an approach to reading was a focus for extensive research in the 1980s (Palincsar and Brown, 1984). It is now becoming more popular in both primary and secondary contexts in the United Kingdom. The approach focuses on developing reading fluency and encouraging autonomy, by defining and modelling the explicit uses of a reading strategy before readers gradually use these skills more independently. The four key strategies identified with this approach are: predict, clarify, question and summarise. In order for readers to develop independence and autonomy, it is suggested that teachers describe and model the strategy before pupils begin to use it independently.

Activity

Identify a non-fiction text which can be used within the Key Stage 2 classroom. This book needs to be one you are familiar with or have studied at depth prior to the activity.

Create a range of questions using the stems below in order to identify different ways to interrogate a text:

What ...?

How does ... know ...?

What does the word ... mean here?

Find one word which shows ...

Explain why ...

What impressions do you get of ...? Use evidence to support your answer.

According to the text, why ...?

Which sentence best summarises the text (four options given)?

It is important to encourage further, deeper reading for those pupils who are already fluent readers and this includes inferring accurately from a range of increasingly sophisticated texts through a range of approaches. In the case study below, Ruby's experience in Year 6 and Year 7 is considered in relation to developing 'mastery in reading' as she became a confident and enthusiastic reader.

Case study: mastering reading through reading a range of texts

Ruby is a twelve-year-old Year 7 pupil coming to the end of her first year at secondary school. She has been a voracious reader since she began to read at the age of four. She explained that the reason she reads so much is to gain knowledge and because fiction texts can be so immersive. The variety afforded by each text read and the wide range of genres can be exciting. Ruby's primary and secondary schools both subscribe to Accelerated Reader (definition to follow below), which monitors pupils' reading and prescribes a level for them so that there is a challenge attached. Ruby thrived with the challenge of monitoring how many millions of words she had read, but she also questioned why it was important to know how many words had been read when it was more important to think about how she was reading the text and what she might be taking from the book.

$\longrightarrow$

While in Year 6, Ruby took responsibility helping with the school library which enabled her to talk about book choices with younger pupils, read with them and see the variety of books available for learners across the school community. She also participated as a reader in the Leeds Book Awards, where children read the fiction texts shortlisted for the children's fiction prize, discuss them in school and provide feedback on each of them. She joined a virtual book group which asks young people to read and review newly published fiction online. These activities tapped into an interest which already existed and as Ruby articulated, it is important that teachers 'don't force it'.

While in primary school, Ruby understood the importance of reading a text in different ways and felt that quite a lot of time in reading sessions focused on identifying important textual features and considering inferences she should make. This was inevitable given the Year 6 SATs test papers. Year 7 has proved to be something of a revelation as she now feels that she is asked more openly 'What do you think?' about texts she has read. Discussion is encouraged in order that she might appreciate different ways to interpret and engage with ideas around authorial intent. With nearly five years before another set of external examinations, it seems that the capacity for more freedom, creativity and discussion is having a positive impact on her as a reader.

This case study shows that more open-ended questioning and discussion as well as exposure to a range of more challenging texts can be beneficial for confident readers. It is also important to acknowledge that many pupils will still need scaffolding in the questioning being used, particularly as they head towards their externally marked Year 6 reading test.

Activity

Review the 2019 KS2 Reading SATs paper. These are readily available on the gov.uk website.

Complete the paper and mark your answers using the guidance pack.

Consider the range of questions for the pupils.

The Accelerated Reader programme

Accelerated Reader is a programme published by Renaissance used in over 40,000 schools worldwide (covering more than 60 countries). Use of technology enables each child to be assessed on their reading ability and then be given a ZPD (zone of proximal development), a term which stems from Vygotsky's original work (1978). It provides a range into which texts of appropriate difficulty are placed. Children can choose any book from their identified 'range' to read. Once the book has been read, the student is prompted to complete an online test to check their knowledge and understanding of the text. The programme also allows them to track the number of words they have read, and they move through the range so texts become increasingly difficult as their reading capacity develops.

There are many advantages to such a system which harnesses the power of technology to 'fine tune' children's independent reading choices. Pupils can respond positively to the competitive element of quizzes once they have finished a book, and teams of readers can also be encouraged to compete over total number of words read. In addition, children become autonomous in their own reading choices and are able to choose texts of a particular genre or by specific authors which are most likely to appeal. This system is not without its challenges, however. It is very difficult to nurture discussions between children about texts when each child may be reading a different book. The quizzing system does not reveal a pupil's personal response to a text, so further activity would be needed to encourage the articulation of 'big ideas'. Finally, teacher input and guidance remain essential in order that pupils are encouraged to choose 'suitable' and appropriately challenging books.

Opportunities to initiate pupils into wider reading communities

The school or local library can enable wider participation so that pupils become more aware of the reading communities which exist beyond the school classroom. This then encourages children to see reading as an activity which can accompany them through life. Ofsted's analysis of research (2013) reinforced the importance of this, suggesting that at secondary level successful schools would 'ensure that the librarian had an important role in developing reading' (2013, p40). As pupils move from primary to secondary school, they may have less structured contact with the school library, so community libraries may bridge the gap and offer some continuity for them. On a wider scale, a children's BBC book club can be accessed through the website. Children are encouraged to get involved by sending in 'reviews, comments, questions, drawings, suggestions and book selfies!' (BBC, 2020). In a similar way, children might be encouraged to swap books with each other in order to nurture the kind of wider dialogue associated with texts and the key themes that arise within them.

Providing space and time for debate and discussion

Personal engagement and enjoyment of reading might be encouraged further through the framing of questions to consider 'What do you think?' While this moves away from the more regulated fact- or inference-based questions of the Key Stage 2 SATs test, such open questions allow the reading of texts through a different lens. For example, Ruby, in her first week at secondary school, was given three extracts from gothic texts to read. She was then asked to identify which of the extracts she felt was most convincingly 'gothic' in style and explain the reasons for her choice. This reading approach asked for a personal response, since two pupils might reach different conclusions but present equally valid explanations. Such an activity really focuses on 'What do you think?' rather than the more straightforward questions around 'What can you infer?' The reader response view of literary criticism is then seen as key, so that interpretation relies upon individual readings.

The United Kingdom Literacy Association has produced position papers about the curriculum and suggest in 'An Alternative Curriculum for English' (2016) that 'Pupils have regular opportunities to discuss their reading with other pupils and with the teacher, articulating their responses to what they have read, and listening carefully to the responses of others' (UKLA, 2016, p12). The importance of oracy in the primary classroom is promoted by Robin Alexander, who led an extensive research project around dialogic teaching which saw improvements in attainment based on a shift to this mode of teaching in Year 5 (Education Endowment Foundation, 2017).

Within the primary classroom at upper Key Stage 2 teachers want to see that children are enthusiastic and personally engaged in the reading they are undertaking. The degree to which this will be the case will depend on both the texts that have been chosen and the pedagogical approach used to explore these texts.

Case study: further activities and teaching strategies that nurture developing readers

In 2019, Calverley Church of England Primary School in Leeds developed an innovative approach to reading with the whole-class text method. Underpinning this system are the beliefs that all children need to meet challenging whole texts and that vocabulary development is absolutely key. Exposure to ambitious vocabulary is essential for children both as readers and writers, but as children progress through primary school and reading independence develops, they are less likely to have a caregiver reading a book to them at home. The whole-class reader is a way for the teacher to model fluent reading to children with twenty minutes of dedicated reading per day in class, as well as exercises to practise retrieval skills, explore vocabulary and predict what might happen next. Pupils are freed up to concentrate on the text without any anxiety about whether they will be asked to read.

In his Year 6 class, the English subject lead Chris Minett's pupils were empowered by being able to choose the text they read. They read the blurbs of three possible texts (but did not see the covers!) and voted to discover the preferred choice. The class chose *Holes* by Louis Sachar, favouring the blurb to this novel over *Cogheart* by Peter Bunzl and *Nevermoor* by Jessica Townsend. Reading did not take place as you might expect at the end of the school

→

day: in order to ensure engagement, it happened either in the morning or straight after lunch. Retrieval practice became gradually more challenging and it was often the less enthusiastic readers who responded most accurately as their confidence grew. A word wall evolved which charted the unusual vocabulary choices which had been encountered and mixed-ability partner work allowed discussion of the text and exploration of increasingly complex ideas about it. During class questioning and discussion sessions, it was essential for the teacher to be responsive to the interests and comprehension level of the children. In addition to the dedicated reading sessions, two reading lessons would focus on this fiction text. For the other three reading lessons, the focus would be a range of non-fiction texts to ensure that children had a varied reading diet in addition to enjoying their complete fiction text.

Focus was on creating excitement and engagement around the text, so there were displays around school about the texts for each class. The high levels of pupil engagement in these books were easily measured by the audible groans when it was time to stop reading each day. A major benefit of this approach is the capacity for pupils to grow in confidence as they develop increasingly sophisticated inference skills while progressing further into the text. More sophisticated analysis was possible given the scale of the text being read, which smaller extracts don't allow. As pupils became immersed in the longer fiction text, their confidence and enthusiasm for reading increased and was evident through engagement while reading and animation seen during discussion.

The National Curriculum for Years 5 and 6 expects an 'increasingly wide range of fiction, poetry, plays, non-fiction and reference books or text books' (DfE, 2013a, p44) and also suggests that children should 'meet books and authors that they might not choose to read themselves' (DfE, 2013a, p45). This creates a dilemma for many teachers. Children will often focus in their own reading habits on a particular genre or specific writer whereas the National Curriculum states that there is an expectation that children have an exposure to a wide range of text types. This case study offers a solution to the problem of knowing how to provide breadth of coverage while still enabling sufficiently detailed coverage of a text to nurture engagement and to allow pupils to feel immersed in the text.

Activity

1. Make a list of all the teaching strategies used in the above case study that you could transfer into your own setting.
2. Read the following two openings to novels about the Second World War and have a go at each of the approaches at the bottom of the page overleaf:

(Continued)

Carrie's War by Nina Bawden

Carrie had often dreamed about coming back. In her dreams she was twelve years old again; short scratched legs in red socks and scuffed, brown sandals, walking along the narrow, dirt path at the side of the railway line to where it plunged down, off the high ridge, through the Druid's Grove. The yew trees in the Grove were dark green and so old that they had grown twisted and lumpy, like arthritic fingers. And in Carrie's dream, the fingers reached out for her, plucking at her hair and her skirt as she ran. She was always running by the end of this dream, running away from the house, uphill towards the railway line.

Goodnight, Mr Tom by Michelle Magorian

'Yes,' said Tom bluntly, on opening the front door.

'What d'you want?'

A harassed middle-aged woman in a green coat and felt hat stood on his step. He glanced at the armband on her sleeve. She gave him an awkward smile.

'I'm the billeting officer for this area,' she began.

'Oh yes, and what's that got to do wi' me?'

She flushed slightly, 'Well, Mr, Mr ...'

'Oakley. Thomas Oakley.'

'Ah, thank you, Mr Oakley.' She paused and took a deep breath. 'Mr Oakley, with the declaration of war imminent ...'

Tom waved his hand. 'I knows all that. Git to the point. What d'you want?' He noticed a small boy at his side.

'It's him I've come about,' she said. 'I'm on my way to your village hall with the others.'

'What others?'

Approach 1:	Approach 2:
Pupils are asked the following questions:	Pupils are asked to think, pair and share the following questions:
1. What did Carrie wear as a twelve-year-old?	1. Which of the novel openings do you find most effective and why?
2. How does the writer present Druid's Grove?	
3. Provide one example of a simile in extract one.	2. What questions have arisen for you as a reader about each text?
4. In the second extract, find and copy one word which shows that the billeting officer is not enjoying the work she is doing.	
5. What impressions do you get of Tom Oakley? Use evidence from the text to support your answer.	

> She stepped to one side. Behind the large iron gate which stood at the end of the graveyard were a small group of children. Many of them were filthy and very poorly clad. Only a handful had a blazer or coat. They all looked bewildered and exhausted. One tiny dark-haired girl in the front was hanging firmly on to a new teddy-bear.

Approach 1 might provide a view of whether children have fully understood the texts and is a way in which their confidence might be developed as they recognise their ability to identify and explain important elements of the text. It could be that after the more precise and closed questions of approach 1, children can then be encouraged to explore a valid personal response. For approach 2, the questions are 'open' in their nature and are likely to encourage discussion and debate. The pupils are 'allowed' to choose whichever opening they prefer if they can explain their choice. Nevertheless, pupils might notice elements without direct instruction such as the use of third person narrative in each extract, use and impact of direct speech and effect of imagery on the reader. Similarly, asking pupils to identify questions which have arisen allows them to predict and anticipate what might happen next. In order to do this, they are inevitably inferring from the text.

How can transition between primary and secondary school preserve a reading culture?

In the early 2000s, the National Literacy Strategy introduced transition units for pupils to follow at the end of Year 6 and in the first few weeks of Year 7 as they moved to secondary school. The English scheme saw pupils reading *Kensuke's Kingdom* and *The Butterfly Lion* by Michael Morpurgo. While the rationale behind this unit was to encourage the preservation of a reading focus and allow a smooth transition to secondary school, the unit was not without problems. Not all schools had covered the material in precisely the same way so the experience became disjointed for some pupils. A positive suggestion from this unit, however, which is still used in many primary schools today, was the use of 'reading journals' to encourage pupils to sustain their reading momentum and record their reading patterns and perceptions. As identified within the transition unit, the open-ended nature of such journals can be hugely beneficial to pupils as: 'Journals can provide pupils with an opportunity to speculate, explore, play with ideas, and be tentative and uncertain in their responses' (DfES, 2002, p19).

Case study: maintaining engagement and promoting an excellent reading culture in secondary school

At Benton Park Secondary School in Leeds there is a keen awareness of the need to promote reading so that all pupils thrive. The Key Stage 3 long-term plan identifies a key purpose of English as to encourage 'empathetic readers'; underpinning this is the principle that as readers we need to understand what texts mean and to 'see how powerful language can be in the texts we study'. The Head of English Lynn Wearing explained a transition project introduced this year designed to encourage incoming Year 7 pupils to view reading positively. A group of Year 11 male pupils from the school went to visit some Year 6 boys in order to act as role models and to promote reading. Together, they read a short story and worked on some creative writing. This focus on role models continues with the well-established practice of sixth form pupils mentoring younger pupils and hearing them read each week, discussing the texts and identifying unfamiliar vocabulary within the text. The impact of both these strategies has been described as 'transformational'. For example, those Year 7 students who had reading mentors made 1.2 years' reading progress on average over seven months, in comparison to their peers who made eight months' progress (according to Accelerated Reader).

Another reading project being embedded in the school is reading a whole fiction text during form time. Pupils enjoy the reading of a whole fiction text, with emphasis being placed on sharing stories and developing a community of readers which is not confined to teachers within the English department. Choices for Year 8 tutor groups include *The Outsiders* by S.E. Hinton, *The Curious Incident of the Dog in the Nighttime* by Mark Haddon, *Liar and Spy* by Rebecca Stead and *The Terrible Thing that Happened to Barnaby Brocket* by John Boyne.

The spotlight on reading has become embedded through regular use of the library, dedicated time for reading during English lessons, use of Accelerated Reader in school and whole-school professional development focused on vocabulary and reading. The importance of whole-school responsibility for creating a literate and reading community is emphasised through this professional development which has encouraged discussion of how to read texts and introduce pupils to more challenging tier two and three vocabulary through reading strategies. The whole-school vocabulary focus has been called 'Word Revolution' and each department has a wordsmith who focuses on its inclusion within the subject's curriculum.

The impact of these strategies has been seen across the school as a whole. All members of staff see it as their responsibility to raise the status of reading and promote vocabulary development. The school has developed a community of readers and the most significant change was seen in low-ability students, where the school has a strategy of reading age-appropriate books to them (for example, *Wonder* by R.J. Palacio and *The Hunger Games* by Suzanne Collins).

Learning outcomes review

After reading this chapter you should now be able to identify:

- how children's reading can be nurtured through the use of challenging texts as they move into upper Key Stage 2;
- what approaches and activities can best be employed in order to nurture developing readers;
- how a reading culture can be preserved in the transition from primary to secondary school.

Conclusion

There is no definitive 'solution' to nurturing reading fluency and encouraging readers to thrive, but this chapter has highlighted a range of ways in which to promote enjoyment of reading in the classroom and beyond. As children move into Key Stage 2 it is important that they continue to develop fluency and confidence through talk in the classroom, modelled reading and structured comprehension approaches. Use of the various reading domains assessed at the end of Key Stage 2 can enable pupils to access and respond to texts in a range of ways. Once pupils are confident and engaged independent readers, it is important to maintain their reading momentum by offering wider opportunities that initiate them into a community of readers which exists beyond the scope of their classroom. In order to nurture these developing readers, we considered strategies around a whole-class fiction text and the way in which reading responses can be both tightly focused and more open-ended to allow exploratory discussion around unknown texts. While research suggests that children's reading declines as they move to secondary school (Ofsted, 2012), there are ways in which reading enthusiasm can continue to be encouraged. Journals and transition units provide opportunities for the primary and secondary cultures to connect, as well as the promotion of reading through mentoring and specific reading projects. Libraries in both contexts can provide a continuity and a means by which independent reading can be encouraged to thrive.

References

BBC (2020) CBBC Book Club. Available at: https://www.bbc.co.uk/cbbc/shows/cbbc-book-club (accessed 16 September 2020).

Bleiman, B. (2020) *What Matters in English Teaching: Collected Blogs and Other Writing*. London: English and Media Centre.

Department for Education (2013) *The National Curriculum in England: Key Stages 1 and 2 Framework Document*. Available at: https://www.gov.uk/government/publications/national-curriculum-in-england-primary-curriculum (accessed 30 April 2020).

Department for Education (DfE) (2014a) *Primary National Curriculum*. Available at: https://www.gov.uk/government/publications/national-curriculum-in-england-primary-curriculum (accessed 21 August 2020).

Department for Education (2014b) *Secondary National Curriculum*. Available at: https://www.gov.uk/government/publications/national-curriculum-in-england-secondary-curriculum (accessed 21 August 2020).

Department for Education and Skills (DfES) (2002) 'Transition from year 6 to year 7 English: Units of Work' from The National Literacy Strategy London: DfES.

Education Endowment Foundation (2017) *Improving Literacy in Key Stage Two*. London: Education Endowment Foundation.

Hall, C. (2015) Understanding reading, in S. Brindley and B. Marshall (eds), *Masterclass in English Education: Transforming Teaching and Learning*. London: Bloomsbury.

National Literacy Trust (2019) *Annual Literacy Survey*. Available at: https://literacytrust.org.uk/research-services/research-reports/children-and-young-peoples-reading-in-2019/ (accessed 21 August 2020).

Ofsted (2012) *Research Evidence on Reading for Pleasure*. Available at: https://www.gov.uk/government/publications/research-evidence-on-reading-for-pleasure (accessed 21 August 2020).

Ofsted (2013) *Improving Literacy in Secondary Schools: A Shared Responsibility*. Available at: https://www.gov.uk/government/publications/improving-literacy-in-secondary-schools-a-shared-responsibility (accessed 21 August 2020).

Ofsted (2019) *Education Inspection Framework*. Available at: https://www.gov.uk/government/publications/education-inspection-framework (accessed 21 August 2020).

Palincsar, A. and Brown, A. (1984) *Reciprocal Teaching of Comprehension-Fostering and Comprehension Monitoring Activities*. Champaign: University of Illinois, Center for Study of Reading.

UKLA (2016) *The Essentials of English*. UKLA: University of Leicester. Available at: https://www.nate.org.uk/wp-content/uploads/2020/02/The-Essentials-of-English-1.pdf (accessed 21 August 2020).

Vygotsky, L. (1978) *Mind in Society: The Development of Higher Mental Processes*. Cambridge, MA: Harvard University Press.

Further materials to deepen your understanding of developing a love of reading in upper Key Stage 2 and Key Stage 3

Times Educational Supplement (2015) 100 fiction books to read before leaving primary. Available at: https://www.tes.com/news/100-fiction-books-read-leaving-primary (accessed 21 August 2020).

For strategies for developing readers in secondary schools see:

Jolliffe, W., Waugh, D. and Beverton, S. (2014) *Supporting Secondary Readers*. London: SAGE.

National Literacy Trust (https://literacytrust.org.uk/) provides current research around.

4 The Creative Curriculum: Encouraging Reading for Pleasure through Art and the Humanities

Lucy M. Davies

Learning outcomes

By reading this chapter you will have considered:

- how a cross-curricular approach can motivate children in reading;
- the meaning of 'creative reading' and 'critical reading';
- how Art and Humanities subjects provide a context for different enhancing different types of reading skills.

Teachers' Standards

3. Demonstrate good subject and curriculum knowledge:

- have a secure knowledge of the relevant subject(s) and curriculum areas, foster and maintain pupils' interest in the subject, and address misunderstandings;
- demonstrate a critical understanding of developments in the subject and curriculum areas, and promote the value of scholarship.

4. Plan and teach well-structured lessons:

- impart knowledge and develop understanding through effective use of lesson time;
- promote a love of learning and children's intellectual curiosity;
- contribute to the design and provision of an engaging curriculum within the relevant subject area(s).

Curriculum link

6.3 Teachers should develop pupils' reading and writing in all subjects to support their acquisition of knowledge. Pupils should be taught to read fluently, understand extended prose (both fiction and non-fiction) and be encouraged to read for pleasure. Schools should do everything to promote wider reading. They should provide library facilities and set ambitious expectations for reading at home (DfE, 2013, p10).

Introduction

Encouraging children to read for pleasure (RfP) has been part of wider initiatives to raise literacy levels in the United Kingdom, and elsewhere, over the last several decades. Research strongly supports the assumption that children who enjoy reading have better learning outcomes and schools have therefore understandably devoted a good deal of curriculum time to reading (DfE, 2012). Meanwhile, with reading being formally assessed in Year 2 and Year 6 SATS tests, the ability to read to an expected standard, whether pleasurable or not, can have short-, medium- and long-term effects on learners, including how they perceive themselves as readers or non-readers (Clark, 2008). Yet, despite initiatives, still we find that many children do not RfP. A recent focus on providing a 'broad and balanced curriculum' (DfE, 2014) and Ofsted 'deep dives' into foundation subjects has led many practitioners to ponder over how best to teach a wide range of subjects at a high standard, while leaving sufficient time to continue trying to fostering a love of reading.

A sensible approach is to provide for reading opportunities when delivering some of the foundation subjects. Using a cross-curricular approach in this way is nothing new, and some excellent ideas for integrating reading with other subjects can be found in research which pre-dates current National Curriculum, including Lyle's 'Enhancing literacy through geography in upper primary classrooms' (2000) and Schleppegrell *et al.*'s 'Literacy in history' (2008). As well as being a practical solution to maximising curriculum time devoted to reading, a cross-curricular approach can provide a relevant and interesting context to encourage reading, while also helping children meet subject-specific aims. As Clark and Rumbold (2006) point out, research suggests that RfP increases:

- general knowledge (e.g. Cunningham and Stanovich, 1998);
- understanding of other cultures (Meek, 1991);
- community participation (e.g. Bus, van Ijzendoorm and Pellegrini, 1995);
- insight into human nature and decision-making (Bruner, 1996).

Such benefits have clear links to art and the humanities. A cross-curricular approach can also provide opportunities for both creative learning and creative teaching, both of which have been linked to higher levels of enjoyment, engagement and achievement (Ofsted, 2011). However, teaching using a cross-curricular approach can present challenges. While reading can be embedded across the curriculum, it is worth remembering that discrete subjects have their own sets of skills and competencies which must be developed. For instance, giving children a comprehension task based on a piece of writing set during the First World War is not an activity which fosters historical skills, it is simply an English lesson which may leave children a small amount of residual knowledge on the conflict. Meeting the aims of the National Curriculum's Programme of Study for History (DfE, 2014) – or other foundation subjects – while also developing children's reading skills requires more complex planning and delivery. Doing so requires a sufficient level of subject knowledge which may present a challenge to teachers (Eaude, 2018), particularly with changes to the content of the Geography and History programmes in recent years.

Despite these challenges, many opportunities to develop RfP lie in a using a cross-curricular approach. Pupils who are highly engaged in a wide range of reading activities are more likely than other pupils to be effective learners and to perform well at school (OECD, 2011, p1). This chapter explores how incorporating creative reading activities across subjects can help engage children by providing varied context which resonates with children, particularly those not naturally inclined to be motivated to read for pleasure. This chapter discusses how art and the humanities can be used to:

- motivate children to read;
- promote particular types of creative and critical reading skills;
- provide opportunities for creative teaching; and
- broaden the range of books and subsequently topics discussed in class.

Research focus: the resurgence of a cross-curricular approach

Taking a cross-curricular approach to teaching and learning is now commonplace, but it has a history of being surprisingly divisive among educators and academics alike. As Hayes (2010, pp381–87) points out, while some hale it as the 'holy grail' of pedagogy, others believe it is a 'poisoned chalice'.

The benefits of a cross-curricular approach were lauded following the publication of the Plowden Report in 1967. In theory, this approach should have worked well; after all, outside education our lives are not compartmentalised into individual 'subjects' and 'disciplines' (Barnes, 2018). However, following a damning report on the quality of teaching in primary schools by HMI in 1978, cross-curricular teaching became associated with an unfocused topic-based curriculum, which was heavily criticised by HMI. A move away from the approach continued with the introduction of a National Curriculum in 1988, the curriculum being planned in discrete subject areas.

Over the last twenty years, a number of influential reports have seen a resurgence in using a cross-curricular approach. The first was *All Our Futures*, commonly known as the Robinson report (National Advisory Committee, 1999), which extolled the virtues of incorporating creative opportunities into the curriculum while arguing for parity between subjects. Subsequent reports, including *The Rose Review* (2006) and *The Cambridge Primary Review* (Alexander, 2010), also suggested a cross-curricular approach may be beneficial, the former specifically referring to reading pedagogy.

→

Currently, many terms are found to describe cross-curricular teaching – for example, 'projects', 'integrated teaching' and 'thematic teaching' (Greenwood, 2013). Considering that constructivist learning theories largely underpin our current educational system, using a pedagogy which encourages children to make links between their learning in different subjects thus becomes more meaningful (Duerr, 2008).

Motivating children to engage with reading

Some children seem to be natural readers, intrinsically motivated to seek out opportunities to read and engaging with a variety of texts. Traditionally, intrinsic rather than extrinsic motivation predicts RfP (e.g. Cox and Guthrie, 2001; Wang and Guthrie, 2004), but the line between intrinsic and extrinsic motivation is often blurred. While some research suggests that personality traits make some children more inclined to engage than others (Rotgans and Schmidt, 2011; Stodd, 2012; Hodge et al., 2018), it is likely that such children have also been nurtured (consciously or subconsciously) to read through exposure to books at home and positive attitudes to reading (Chakravarthy, 2011; van Bergen et al., 2017). These environmental factors can act as extrinsic motivators – that is, children wanting to please their parents, who are avid readers, by adopting similar habits.

What is clear is that better readers tend to read more because they are motivated to read, which leads to improved vocabulary and better skills. Without finding a way to motivate all primary-aged children to RfP, it becomes increasingly difficult to mitigate the so-called 'Matthew Effect' (Stanovich, 1986), where the gap between the better and poorer readers continues to widen. One way to motivate children to read is show them that reading has a purpose. A relevant purpose will vary from child to child depending on their different experiences and backgrounds, as well as varying levels and types of motivation (Ryan and Deci, 2000). The 'real-world' contexts of art and humanities subjects can provide pupils with a sense of personal relevance when reading. As Stewart and Walker explain: 'Students need to see the connection of school subject areas to the real world, but also that these subject areas are connected to one another' (Stewart and Walker, 2005, p13).

Art and the humanities also help teachers and children move away from the tendency to measure reading ability through assessment data, which can lead to teachers labelling children according to their 'ability' (Hempel-Jorgensen et al., 2017, p6). A more holistic approach to gauging children's reading ability can guide teachers and children away from lowering their expectations. Art is seen as an accessible, open-ended subject and often cited by children as one of the most enjoyable curriculum areas. For children who are not confident readers, it provides a safe context to introduce the skills necessary for enjoying and comprehending text. Images can be used to develop children's inference skills and as stimuli to discuss imagery and meaning. Comprehension skills can also be explored through images before, or alongside, practising the same skill with text. The humanities allow for children's spiritual, moral, social and cultural (SMSC) development and often cover subject matters which lead to deep thinking and thought-provoking discussion. Meanwhile, the breadth of potential topics across these subjects enables teachers to make choices based on what they feel will engage their particular group of learners, while still meeting the aims of the programme of study, something they are often unable to do in the core subjects.

My chapter in *Mastering Writing at Greater Depth* (edited by Bushnell *et al.*) explained how different materials can be used to engage children in writing (Davies, 2020). Similarly, art and humanities can provide various genres of material to stimulate children's love of reading. Research has concluded that a successful classroom library should include a wide range of categories of reading materials, for example:

- stories and narrative accounts, e.g. fairy tales, folk tales and biographies;
- picture books with thought-provoking images and examples of artistic talent;
- information books;
- computers with bookmarked Web pages, including major reference sources;
- miscellaneous reading materials, such as popular magazines, newspapers, catalogues, recipe books, encyclopaedia.

(Reutzel *et al.*, 2004, p7)

At a time when school budgets do not allow for mass-spending, teachers are required to think creatively about how to access such a range of texts. Incorporating a variety of reading materials can introduce a sense of novelty to reading which, in turn, can lead to engagement. Choice is also more likely to stimulate children's creative thinking and a range of material can be particularly useful for encouraging boys to read more and help close the ongoing gender gap when it comes to RfP, which is well-documented in the literature (Clark and Foster, 2005; Clark *et al.*, 2005). Although the gap may be narrowing slightly (ROGO, 2018), it remains a concern. Research has also found that boys have a tendency to prefer non-fiction texts (Kirsch *et al.*, 2002; Merga, 2017). Fact retrieval activities are well-suited to geography, history and citizenship and present an opportunity to coax children into reading, by setting a challenge based on research activity. It has also been found that RfP declines with age, particularly as children finish primary school and move through secondary school (Topping, 2010; Clark and Douglas, 2011). Introducing children to thought-provoking and challenging reading materials which deal with issues such as climate change, bullying and racial equality through history, citizenship and religious studies in upper Key Stage 2 can help sustain their engagement in reading, while also shaping them as a tolerant and respectful learner.

Activity

To begin maximising opportunities to incorporate reading in art and the humanities:

- look at the next topics you will be delivering in art and the humanities subjects;
- identify the key subject-specific aims children need to meet;
- consider what opportunities there are within these topics to embed active reading opportunities that will develop children's creative and critical reading skills.

For inspiration, you may find it useful to look at 'Practical approaches 2' towards the bottom of the Historical Association webpage on 'Cross-curricular learning'. You will see hyperlinks to a variety of topics with ideas for lessons with strong literacy and history links.

https://www.history.org.uk/primary/module/3638/leading-primary-history/3653/cross-curricular-learning

Fostering creative and critical reading skills

As well as motivating children to read, art and humanities subjects provide many opportunities to enhance children's creative reading skills (these are discussed subject by subject later in the chapter). But what exactly is 'creative reading'? Whereas 'creative writing' is a familiar term to primary school teachers, creative reading is a less-used phrase. Attracting some interest in the 1970s and 1980s (Labuda, 1974; Nash and Torrence, 1974; Boothby, 1980), it seemed to disappear from popular use before making a welcomed, but low-key reappearance in the last decade (Small and Arnone, 2011; Yurdakal, 2019). Creative reading has been defined as:

> Reading for implied and inferred meanings, appreciative reactions, and critical evaluation. The act of critical reading goes beyond literal comprehension to demand that the reader produce fresh, original ideas not explicitly stated in the reading material. The reader becomes an active participant and adds to what the author has written.

> (Adams, 1968, p1)

Inferring meaning from a painting; interpreting historical sources; discussing the morals of a story in religious studies; thinking of what gives their locality a sense of identity in geography; and imagining what life would have been like in a particular historical era are all activities which require children to think creatively. Incorporating reading activities with the humanities can therefore allow for more varied and imaginative learning and teaching (Padgett, 1996).

However, not only do children need to be able to generate ideas through creative thinking, but they also need to critique them in order to make informed predictions and valid explanations. For instance, children may read a variety of sources about why Stonehenge was built and creative thinking will help them make connections between the sources, possibly resulting in them having their own theory. The next step is for them to determine the suitability of their ideas and assess which of the sources they find most convincing. This requires critical reading skills.

More than any other generation of children, today's pupils need to be encouraged in developing critical reading skills. In 1999 the International Reading Association predicted:

> Adolescents entering the adult world in the 21st century will read and write more than at any other time in human history. They will need advanced levels of literacy to perform their jobs, run their households, act as citizens, and conduct their personal lives. They will need literacy to cope with the flood of information they will find everywhere they turn.

> (International Reading Association, 1999, p3)

This prediction appears to be proving correct, although what could not be foreseen was that much of the 'flood of information' would come in the form of so-called 'fake news'. Not only do children now need to be able to read and comprehend text, they also need to be able to make an informed assessment of how reliable it is. These literacy skills, so relevant to contemporary life, can be developed when learners are encouraged to 'adopt critical perspectives toward texts such as songs, poems, novels, conversations, pictures and movies' (Aslan, 2016, p1798). In doing so, reading becomes much less of a passive action and requires children to actively engage, as critical reading relies not only on information but also on different ways of thinking about the subject matter (Knott, n.d., p1).

Subject content in art and the humanities can allow for culturally relevant reading opportunities associated with interpretation and digesting new ideas. These are useful in stimulating interesting discussion, and include 'social subjects and institutions significant to students' lives, like family, government, equality, social justice, racism, poverty' (Aslan, 2016, p1798). In addition, developing children as critical readers allows them to evaluate text from numerous angles including logical, rhetorical, historical, ethical, social and personal perspectives (Wheeler, 2007), thus preparing them for life beyond the classroom.

Teachers' role

So far, this chapter has discussed how and why children's reading can be developed through art and humanities by encouraging pupils to thinking creatively and critically. But a cross-curricular approach to reading also allows for, in fact demands, creative teaching. As mentioned previously, teachers may need to think creatively in terms of sources for a variety of reading materials, which can present challenges. Teachers may also want to use an art or humanities topic as a theme to recreate an immersive reading environment which is relevant to the children. Visits can also be used as a way to consolidate and expand children's understanding of a cross-curricular topic (see case study). Even in preparing for a visit, creative reading opportunities can emerge – for example, children finding out information to help them plan a visit, such as opening times, current exhibitions and places on site to eat.

Successful integration of reading opportunities across art and humanities also requires teachers to be creative in terms of:

- identifying topics which learners will respond to emotionally and cognitively;
- making links between reading activities and subject content;
- thinking of efficient (cost- and time-effective) ways to develop their art and humanities subject knowledge;
- predicting difficult questions which may arrive (particularly when dealing with potentially controversial or sensitive topics);
- thinking on the spot if a lesson takes an unexpected turn, in order to follow children's creative thinking and ideas.

Assessing creative and critical reading also requires teachers to be creative, even if done informally. However, in doing so, both pupils and teachers avoid restrictively measuring attainment in reading through tests, which has been called 'the coldest of all instruments' (Padgett, 1996, p16).

Case study: history

At John Emmerson Batty Primary School in Redcar, it was decided to dedicate a whole term to one history topic in order to maximise opportunities for integrating reading with history.

A story with a historical theme is chosen at the beginning of the term on which to base English activities, while the same era is explored in history lessons. During the term children

⟶

also go on an educational visit to a historical site or museum and experience the era first-hand through drama activities.

Rebecca Walker and Julie Norris, who teach in Year 6, read *Street Child* by Berlie Doherty to their class, while delivering history lessons on the Victorians. The cross-curricular approach was found to allow children to develop a deep understanding of the era, and enable them to relate to a fictional character of a similar age, allowing them to think creatively and critically about what life would have been like in Victorian times. During the term, the class visited Beamish Open Air Museum dressed as Victorian children, further allowing them to immerse themselves in the era. Rebecca and Julie found that dedicating a whole term to one topic meant children had the chance to carry out their own research at home, and watch films like *The Secret Garden* and *Oliver!* in their own time. She found that children's enthusiasm for *Street Child* meant they went beyond passive listening and were keen to offer their responses to the text during lessons.

Activity

This activity is designed to help to build a resource bank of books that could be used for whole-class reads, individual lessons or for your classroom library.

Go to the website *Books for Topics* (https://www.booksfortopics.com/) and select Topic Book Lists. You will find a drop down menu where you can select History, Geography, or Other Topics. Explore each section and compile a list of three to five books from each section that you think you could use with your current year group. Use these questions in supporting your choice:

- Does it relate to an upcoming topic I will be teaching?
- Does it deal with a topical issue?
- Does it help explain a sensitive topic?
- Is it age-appropriate for my year group?
- What will the children enjoy about it?
- What sort of questions might it prompt from the class and how will I help answer them?

Creative reading activities to support the delivery of subject-specific skills

As previously mentioned, integral to successfully delivering foundation subjects is having an awareness of their individual aims as stipulated in the National Curriculum (DfE, 2013). Reading can help support some of these outcomes being met, but equally the subject itself can provide a context for teachers hoping to develop particular reading skills. Here, ideas for active reading are discussed in relation to appropriate subject-specific learning outcomes. Of course, while particular skills and competencies may be most closely associated with one subject, there is scope for some of these reading activities to be suitable in other subjects besides those suggested below.

Ideas for art

The visual arts have been recognised as helping develop children's comprehension skills for some time. Comprehension has been described as 'a complex, dynamic and strategic process that involves the reader using prior knowledge about the world, about language and about texts to construct and extract meaning from texts' (Fellowes and Oakley, 2014, p297). However, developing visual literacy can also act as a precursor for interpreting written text and developing inference skills. Therefore, clear links lie between evaluating and analysing creative works (DfE, 2013) and developing reading skills.

Key Stage 1: illustration
Children produce illustrations for an oral story told by the teacher. This allows the teacher to see if children have remembered key elements and the sequence of the story. Illustrations can be in the style of a particular artist, depending on the year group or be produced using particular materials.

Key Stage 2: book-making
Teachers choose a theme which they think will interest the children, or can choose several themes from which the children select one. Children then produce their own picture books, allowing them to think creatively about how to visually represent the theme in question.

Key Stage 1 and 2: interpretation
Teachers show children several pieces of art representing the same event or place. Children can discuss which piece of art they like most and why, before moving on to exploring why artists represent things differently. Older children may be able to make links to events in their own lives, where they remember an event differently from their friends. This introduces children to different perspectives and to the idea that, even with written text, each reader may have a slightly different interpretation of events.

Ideas for history

History is strongly associated with research skills and an enquiry-based learning approach. Retrieving key information on an historical person or event from written sources enables children to develop their scanning and skimming skills. Often there are 'gaps' in evidence requiring readers to engage in 'possibility thinking' to create a plausible narrative. Although such reading skills may sound too sophisticated, Cooper (1995) and Bage (2000) argue that most young children are capable of reconstructing the past from evidence and make unusual imaginative connections (Blake and Edwards, 2012).

Key Stage 1: advertising
Children look at toy adverts from different eras and try to sort them into chronological order. This is an activity which appeals to younger children, while also introducing them to timelines and persuasive texts.

Key Stage 2: decision-making
Rose Blanche, by Christophe Gallaz and Roberto Innocenti, is a thought-provoking fictional picture book for upper Key Stage 2 about a girl who helps prisoners in a concentration camp. It is a very useful text for encouraging children to make predictions about the story, but also in discussing her decision-making. This story can be used as a starting point to discuss the Holocaust and develop children's sense of empathy.

Ideas for geography

Geography has the unenviable label of the worst-taught subject at primary school, with several Ofsted reports finding teachers lack subject knowledge in the subject (Ofsted, 2008; 2011). This poses a problem for using a cross-curricular approach, which is seen by many as requiring a deep level of teacher knowledge. Yet, it is hard to argue with Catling's statement that 'no aspect of geography can really be taught in isolation' (Catling, 2017, p84). Here, several ideas are presented to support engaging geography lessons which also promote reading.

Key Stage 1: treasure hunts
Children learn about key features of maps. They then create their own maps and hide clues around the school which lead to some 'treasure'. Children swap maps and embark on the 'treasure hunt'. Teachers may want to allow children to dress as pirates or explorers to add excitement. Children have a clear purpose for reading as reading the clues is vital in finding the 'treasure'.

Key Stage 2: etymology
Children examine maps of England and look for commonalities between place names, using scanning techniques – for example, towns and cities including 'chester', 'pool' and 'mouth'. They then generate ideas as to what certain names might mean. Not only does this activity help children learn locations of towns and cities, but it can also be used as a starting point to introduce children to the origins and influences on of the English language. This can also be linked to history and the invaders and settlers topic.

Key Stage 2: environmental issues
Children work in groups researching an environmental issue of their choice with the purpose of presenting a PowerPoint to the rest of the class. Using their critical reading skills,

they choose what they think are the most compelling pieces of evidence to use in their presentation.

Ideas for religious education

Religious stories tend to have a clear sense of purpose. Characters are often faced with making important decisions and partake in a spiritual journey. As such, religious tales are useful in familiarising children with narrative structures and discussing characters' thought processes. Visual images and symbolism are also integral to major religions studies at primary school and allow children to develop inference skills.

Key Stage 1 and 2: exploring religious texts

This activity is aimed at developing children's love of and respect for books. Children learn about how followers of particular religions look after their religious texts – for instance, the Qur'an or the Torah. This activity can be linked to history topics such as Anglo-Saxons (Lindisfarne gospels) and ancient civilisations.

Key Stage 2: making links

This activity involves choosing to research festivals from two religions and examining their similarities and differences. The research involved in this task helps build reading stamina, as well as having a clear purpose.

Ideas for citizenship

Citizenship presents a wealth of opportunities to engage children in reading through interesting and sometimes controversial or sensitive subject matters.

EYFS/Key Stage 1: fill your bucket

The teacher reads the whole class *Have You Filled Your Bucket Today?* by Carol McCloud and David Messing, prompting children to discuss what makes them feel happy and sad and what they can do to make their friends feel happy. Children then create their own mini buckets to be hung in the classroom: when a friend does something kind, a paper heart can be added to their bucket. This activity enables children to see that books can reflect their own emotions and promote positive relationships.

Key Stage 2: diversity biographies

This activity involves children researching a famous person who has overcome prejudice and discrimination. Children will need to think about how to gather information about their chosen famous person and then demonstrate criticality in choosing which pieces of information should be included. An excellent book to launch this activity is Cerrie Burnell's *I Am Not a Label: 34 Disabled Artists, Thinkers, Athletes and Activists from Past and Present* (2020).

Key Stage 2: language development and cultural diversity

Encourage children to collect leaflets that have been posted through their doors from local take-away outlets. Working in groups, ask the children to make a list of their favourite foods. Each group shares their lists with the rest of the class and the teacher asks, 'Where do these foods come from?' with the teacher writing suggestions on the white board. Children then explore the menus and find words which they think originate from abroad. This lesson can be used in a series of lessons focusing on positive contributions made to current British culture from immigration.

Learning outcomes review

Now that you have read this chapter, you should understand:

- how a cross-curricular approach to reading can motivate children to read for pleasure;
- why and how art and humanities can provide a suitable context to develop creative and critical reading skills;
- the challenges and benefits of a cross-curricular approach.

Conclusion

To optimise creative opportunities to foster a love of reading through art and the humanities, teachers need to have a clear sense of the type of reading they hope to promote in a particular lesson. This chapter has suggested that particular subjects are natural contexts for particular skills to develop. Meanwhile, the choice of cross-curricular texts teachers make to introduce to their classes can develop not only children's subject-specific content knowledge, but also their sense of individual and collective identity. Literature can provide a safe and sensitive stimulus to discuss particularly emotive topics, particularly in history, religious education and citizenship.

References

Adams, P.J. (1968) *Creative Reading*. Boston: International Reading Association. April 24–27. Available at: https://files.eric.ed.gov/fulltext/ED020090.pdf (accessed 21 August 2020).

Alexander, R. (2010) *Children, their World, their Education: Final Report and Recommendations of the Cambridge Primary Review*. London: Routledge.

Aslan, Y. (2016) The effect of cross-curricular instruction on reading comprehension. *Universal Journal of Educational Research*, 4(8): 1797–801.

Bage, G. (2000) *Thinking History*. Primary Directions series. New York and London: Routledge Falmer, pp4–14.

Barnes, J. (2018) *Applying Cross-Curricular Approaches Creatively*. London: Routledge.

Blake, A. and Edwards, G. (2012) Creativity in history and the humanities, in L. Newton (ed.), *Creativity for a New Curriculum 5–11*. London: Routledge, p80.

Boothby, P.R. (1980) Creative and critical reading for the gifted. *The Reading Teacher*, 33(6): 674–6.

Catling, S. (2017) High quality in primary humanities: insights from the UK's school inspectorates. *Education 3–13*, 45(3): 354–65.

Chakravarthy, G. (1998) *A Study of Reading Patterns Among Primary School Children In Penang*. Universiti Sains Malaysia Project Cooperation, Ministry of Education and the British Council.

Clark, C. (2008) *Britain's Next Top Model*. London: National Literacy Trust.

Clark, C. and Douglas, J. (2011) *Young People's Reading and Writing: An In Depth Study Focusing on Enjoyment, Behaviour, Attitudes and Attainment*. National Literacy Trust. London: ERIC.

Clark, C. and Foster, A. (2005) *Children's and Young People's Reading Habits and Preferences: The Who, What, Why, Where and When*. London: National Literacy Trust.

Clark, C. and Rumbold, K. (2006) *Reading for Pleasure: A Research Overview*. National Literacy Trust. London: ERIC.

Clark, C., Torsi, S. and Strong, J. (2005) *Young People and Reading: A School Study Conducted by the National Literacy Trust for the Reading Champions Initiative*. London: National Literacy Trust.

Cooper, H. (2005) *History in Primary Schools*. London: Institute of Historical Research.

Cox, K.E. and Guthrie, J.T. (2001) Motivational and cognitive contributions to students' amount of reading. *Contemporary Educational Psychology*, 26(1): 116–31.

Davies, L.M. (2020) Engaging pupils through the use of different materials to produce deeper writing, in A. Bushnell, A. Gill and D. Waugh (eds), *Mastering Writing at Greater Depth: A Guide for Primary Teaching*. London: SAGE.

Department for Education (DfE) (2013) *The National Curriculum in England: Key Stages 1 and 2 Framework Document*. Available at: https://www.gov.uk/government/publications/national-curriculum-in-england-primary-curriculum (accessed 30 April 2020).

Department for Education (DfE) (2014) *The National Curriculum in England: Framework for Key Stages 1 to 4*. Available at: https://www.gov.uk/government/publications/national-curriculum-in-england-framework-for-key-stages-1-to-4/the-national-curriculum-in-england-framework-for-key-stages-1-to-4 (accessed 6 October 2020).

DfE Standards Research Team (2012) Research Evidence on Reading for Pleasure Education. Available at: https://assets.publishing.service.gov.uk/government/uploads/system/uploads/attachment_data/file/284286/reading_for_pleasure.pdf (accessed 21 August 2020).

Duerr, L.L. (2008) Interdisciplinary instruction. *Educational Horizons*, 86(3): 173–80.

Eaude, T. (2018) *Developing the Expertise of Primary and Elementary Classroom Teachers: Professional Learning for a Changing World*. London: Bloomsbury.

Fellowes, J., and Oakley, G. (2014) *Language, literacy and early childhood education*, 2nd Ed. Melbourne, Australia: Oxford University Press.

Greenwood, R. (2013) Subject-based and cross-curricular approaches within the revised primary curriculum in Northern Ireland: teachers' concerns and preferred approaches. *Education 3–13*, 41(4): 443–58.

Hayes, D. (2010) The seductive charms of a cross-curricular approach. *Education 3–13*, 38(4): 381–87.

Hempel-Jorgensen, A., Cremin, T., Harris, D. and Chamberlain, L. (2017) *Understanding Boys' (Dis)Engagement with Reading for Pleasure: Project Findings*. Milton Keynes: Open University.

HMI (1978) *Primary Education in England: A Survey by HM Inspectors of Schools*. London: Her Majesty's Stationery Office.

Hodge, B., Wright, B. and Bennett, P. (2018) The role of grit in determining engagement and academic outcomes for university students. *Research in Higher Education*, 59(4): 448–60.

International Reading Association (1999) *High-stakes Assessments in reading: A Position Statement of the International Reading Association*. Newark, DE: International Reading Association.

Kirsch, I., De Jong, J., Lafontaine, D., McQueen, J., Mendelovits, J. and Monseur, C. (2002) *Reading for Change: Performance and Engagement Across Countries: Results of PISA 2000*. Paris: OECD.

Knott, D. (n.d.) *Critical Reading Towards Critical Writing*. Toronto: New College Writing Centre, University of Toronto. Available at: https://advice.writing.utoronto.ca/researching/critical-reading/ (accessed 2 October 2020).

Labuda, M. (1974) *Creative Reading for Gifted Learners: A Design for Excellence*. Michigan: International Reading Association.

Lyle, S. (2000) Enhancing literacy through geography in upper primary classrooms. *International Research in Geographical and Environmental Education*, 9(2), 141-156.

Merga, M. (2017) Do males really prefer non-fiction, and why does it matter? *English in Australia*, 52(1): 27.

Nash, W.R. and Torrance, E.P. (1974) Creative reading and the questioning abilities of young children. *The Journal of Creative Behavior*, 8(1): 15–19.

National Advisory Committee on Creative, Cultural Education (1999) *All Our Futures: Creativity, Culture and Education*. London: DfEE.

OECD (2011) PISA: Do students today read for pleasure? *PISA in Focus*, 8.

Ofsted (2008) *Geography in Schools: Changing Practice*. Available at: https://www.geography.org.uk/download/ofsted%20report%20good%20practice%20in%20schools%20-%20changing%20practice%202008.pdf (accessed 6 October 2020).

Ofsted (2011) *Removing Barriers to Literacy*. Manchester: Ofsted.

Padgett, R. (1996) *Creative Reading: What It Is, How To Do It, and Why*. Illinois: ERIC.

Plowden, B.B.H.P. (1967) *Children and their Primary School: A Report of the Central Advisory Council for Education (England). Vol.1*. London: HMSO.

Reutzel, D.R., Fawson, P. and Fawson, P.C. (2002) *Your Classroom Library: New Ways to give it more Teaching Power*. New York: Scholastic.

ROGO (2018) *Read on. Get on*. Available at: https://literacytrust.org.uk/policy-and-campaigns/read-on-get-on/ (accessed 6 January 2021).

Rose, J. (2006) *Independent Review of the Teaching of Early Reading* (No. 0201-2006DOC-EN). London: DfES.

Rotgans, J.I. and Schmidt, H.G. (2011) Situational interest and academic achievement in the active-learning classroom. *Learning and Instruction*, 21(1): 58–67.

Ryan, R.M. and Deci, E.L. (2000) Intrinsic and extrinsic motivations: classic definitions and new directions. *Contemporary Educational Psychology*, 25(1): 54–67.

Schleppegrell, M., Greer, S. and Taylor, S. (2008) Literacy in history: language and meaning. *Australian Journal of Language and Literacy*, 31.

Small, R.V. and Arnone, M.P. (2011) Creative reading. *Knowledge Quest*, 39(4): 12.

Stanovich, K.E. (1986) Cognitive processes and the reading problems of learning disabled children: evaluating the assumption of specificity. *Psychological and Educational Perspectives on Learning Disabilities*, 19(10): 87–131.

Stewart, M.G. and Walker, R. (2005) *Rethinking Curriculum in Art*. Worcester, MA: Davis.

Stodd, J. (2012) *Exploring the World of Social Learning*. Available at: https://books.google.co.uk/books?hl=en&lr=&id=WN8PBAAAQBAJ&oi=fnd&pg=PT3&dq=Stodd+2012+engagement&ots=pJHgxRtkSQ&sig=9qXtdzVbYqyzXcEgr177uogo99Q&redir_esc=y#v=onepage&q=Stodd%202012%20engagement&f=false (accessed 6 October 2020).

Topping, K.J. (2010) *What Kids are Reading: The Book-Reading Habits of Students in British Schools, 2010*. London: Renaissance Learning UK.

van Bergen, E., van Zuijen, T., Bishop, D. and de Jong, P.F. (2017) Why are home literacy environment and children's reading skills associated? What parental skills reveal. *Reading Research Quarterly*, 52(2): 147–60.

Wang, J.H.Y. and Guthrie, J.T. (2004) Modeling the effects of intrinsic motivation, extrinsic motivation, amount of reading, and past reading achievement on text comprehension between US and Chinese students. *Reading Research Quarterly*, 39(2): 162–86.

Wheeler, L.K. (2007) *Critical Reading of an Essay's Argument*. Available at: http://web.cn.edu/kwheeler/reading_basic.html (accessed 2 October 2020).

Yurdakal, I.H. (2019) Examination of correlation between attitude towards reading and perception of creative reading. *European Journal of Educational Research*, 8(2): 443–52.

5 Reading and the STEM Curriculum

Steve Higgins, Fay Lewis, Rachel Simpson, Jo Smith and David Whitehead

Learning outcomes

By reading this chapter you will:

- learn about the importance and potential of the STEM curriculum for reading;
- see practical examples of how reading can be integrated with science, technology and mathematics;
- develop your knowledge about reading and the wider curriculum.

Teachers' Standards

3. Demonstrate good subject and curriculum knowledge:

- have a secure knowledge of the relevant subject(s) and curriculum areas, foster and maintain pupils' interest in the subject, and address misunderstandings.

4. Plan and teach well-structured lessons:

- impart knowledge and develop understanding through effective use of lesson time;
- promote a love of learning and children's intellectual curiosity;
- contribute to the design and provision of an engaging curriculum within the relevant subject area(s).

Curriculum links

6.1 Teachers should develop pupils' spoken language, reading, writing and vocabulary as integral aspects of the teaching of every subject ... Fluency in the English language is an essential foundation for success in all subjects.

6.3 Teachers should develop pupils' reading and writing in all subjects to support their acquisition of knowledge. Pupils should be taught to read fluently, understand extended prose (both fiction and non-fiction) and be encouraged to read for pleasure.

(Continued)

(Continued)

6.4 Pupils' acquisition and command of vocabulary are key to their learning and progress across the whole curriculum. ... In addition, it is vital for pupils' comprehension that they understand the meanings of words they meet in their reading across all subjects, and older pupils should be taught the meaning of instruction verbs that they may meet in examination questions. It is particularly important to induct pupils into the language which defines each subject in its own right, such as accurate mathematical and scientific language (DfE, 2013, p10).

Introduction

When we think about reading and reading for pleasure, it is fiction that immediately springs to mind. Stories used within science, technology, engineering and mathematics (STEM) can encourage both the act of reading and inspire pupils to improve their knowledge about scientific phenomena, the world of technology and mathematics. If pupils expand their reading for pleasure into the factual world, they open the door to a wealth of information, independently improving their knowledge and developing their vocabulary and their understanding. Having non-fiction books available may also elicit interest from more reluctant readers, and they may experience their first taste of the joy of reading. This wider exposure to the vocabulary and language of these subjects is a vital part of developing children's knowledge and understanding across the curriculum.

Reading for STEM and STEM for reading

STEM subjects (Science, Technology, Engineering and Mathematics) are often perceived as being built on mathematical understanding rather than literacy skills. However, in reality, much of the work of STEM specialists comes from reading, analysing and interpreting the texts of others. Each subject has its own particular vocabulary and ways of writing and reasoning. In addition, the ability to collaborate through well-developed literacy skills is vital; without the ability to read deeply, effective teaching and learning in STEM cannot happen. If we want children to understand the nature of STEM subjects, we need to embed the use of reading as a tool to support learning and enquiry. In this way, a consideration of deeper reading can bring much to the STEM disciplines, but what can STEM bring to reading?

Research focus: STEM

When considering ways to encourage deeper reading, many teachers may not automatically turn to a STEM text. However, where children are reluctant to engage with fiction, alternative texts may be needed (Snow, 2002). We have known for over 70 years that older children often prefer non-fiction (Moss and Hendershot, 2002; Norvell, 1950) and so providing a wide range of text types, including non-fiction STEM texts, is vital in any classroom. Finding a STEM topic that piques interest, and enabling children to select texts focused on these interests for themselves, can motivate them to read. This can be a critical factor in the development of reading processes (Allington, 1994). Reading texts with STEM themes can also be one of the best ways for children to develop the ability to reason with texts (Pearson *et al.*, 2010). The use of such texts can not only lead to enhanced STEM understanding (Cervetti *et al.*, 2012), but also more general vocabulary development (Bortnem, 2011; Marra, 2014) and knowledge regarding how different texts are structured (Palincsar and Magnusson, 2001).

STEM-related non-fiction texts can be difficult for children to interpret as the material is often more challenging, which impedes comprehension (Hoffmann *et al.*, 2015; Duke *et al.*, 2011). Many therefore advocate for a twin-text approach where both fiction and non-fiction books on the same topic are paired together and the content explored in unison, fostering deeper understanding and enjoyment (Dreher and Kletzien, 2015; Camp, 2000). This can be extended to a multitext approach where a variety of texts on similar themes are read together. Such an approach offers multiple entry points for children and exposes them to the use of new vocabulary in different contexts, thus aiding vocabulary acquisition and comprehension (Cervetti *et al.*, 2016; Nagy and Townsend, 2012).

Activity: identifying suitable texts

Select a topic from the science, design and technology or computing and maths aspects of your curriculum and list a variety of related texts appropriate for the age of your class. Below is an example related to space for Key Stage 2 children:

Genre	Example
Fiction or narrative non-fiction	• *I love you Michael Collins* by Lauren Baratz-Logsted • *The Darkest Dark* by Chris Hadfield
Non-fiction	• *Welcome to Mars: Making a Home on the Red Planet* by Buzz Aldrin, with Marianne J. Dyson • *A Hundred Billion Trillion Stars* by Seth Fishman and Isabel Greenberg • *Unlocking the Universe* by Stephen and Lucy Hawking

(Continued)

(Continued)

Genre	Example
Active non-fiction (interactive, includes activities)	• *StarFinder for Beginners* by Maggie Aderin-Pocock • *Astronomy for Kids: How to Explore Outer Space with Binoculars, a Telescope, or Just Your Eyes!* by Bruce Betts
Biography	• *Margaret and the Moon* by Dean Robbins, illustrated by Lucy Knisley • *Grace Hopper: Queen of Computer Code* by Laurie Wallmark
Poetry	• *Blast Off! Poems About Space* by Lee Bennett Hopkins

Case study: STEM

Luke's Year 1 class contains many reluctant readers. However, he uses the children's natural curiosity about the world to engage them with reading by employing a multitext approach. This case study explores how Luke used a rich range of texts about the STEM topic of sounds to give meaning and purpose to reading. In a multitext approach, books do not always have to have a specific STEM theme. In fact, for some of the children in Luke's class, texts containing lots of information and subject-specific language demotivated them and slowed down reading, leading to poor comprehension and engagement. Luke therefore decided to use a fictional text as the basis of their topic, using the story *Peace at Last* by Jill Murphy to pose a STEM-focused challenge.

To use texts as a starting point for STEM challenges children must have a thorough understanding of the content. Usually Luke's class struggled to participate in discussions focused on interpreting and inferring from texts, but when Luke said that they needed to think about Daddy Bear's problem (asking 'How was Daddy Bear feeling?' 'What does he want to happen?' etc.) and how the children could help to solve his problem, they were seen to engage more deeply with such questions, offering more detailed and complex answers. This richer understanding of the story then helped them to pose solutions to the problem.

It would be easy to end the activity here, but Luke continued to engage the children in reading about the topic through a range of texts. Knowing that some of the children in his class were daunted by the prospect of having to read a full book, Luke selected a range of accessible non-fiction books where the children were able select multiple entry points for their reading which allowed them to be in charge of selecting aspects which were most useful to them. Using these texts the children investigated solutions used by others (deciding that bears would rather wear ear defenders than use ear plugs!), the materials used and how they are made. They also continued to draw on a range on fictional texts. For example, after reading *Handa's Noisy Night* by Eileen Browne and digital sources about bears and their habitats they considered which noises bears may hear in the wild. Using *Doctor* by Lucy George (from the

⟶

Busy People range) they considered how people (and bears!) look after their ears, writing questions to ask the doctor about this to help them engage with the content further. This was followed by a STEM-focused activity where the children made and tested out solutions based on what they had read.

The example used in Luke's classroom provides us with some useful ideas about how to use STEM to engage children with texts, motivating children to read and giving their reading purpose.

Curriculum links

Science Year 1:

- distinguish between an object and the material from which it is made;
- identify and name a variety of everyday materials, including wood, plastic, glass, metal, water and rock;
- describe the simple physical properties of a variety of everyday materials;
- compare and group together a variety of everyday materials on the basis of their simple physical properties.

Developing engagement in science

Using science books can help explain and explore contemporary global issues such as the environmental concerns of pollution and global warming. Johnson and Giorgis (2002) recommend *The Case of the Gasping Garbage* by Michele Torrey, where detectives use the principles of science to solve mysteries; there are even experiments for the reader to try. Within primary classrooms we use textbooks to supplement our teaching, but it has been shown that the reading level required to extract information is often above that possessed by the children trying to use them (Bryce, 2011). The vocabulary may be overcomplicated, with wonderfully abstract and conceptual ideas being reduced to dry and boring facts.

Research focus: science

No wonder, then, that Alexander and Jarman (2018) found children expected science books to be difficult and dull, and would not select them if given a choice. If we wish to change their perception, we need to teach children how to use these books. Bryce (2011) suggests a

$\longrightarrow$

guided reading approach, enabling students to develop skills, such as skimming, re-reading and extracting pertinent points. Trickier scientific words can be decoded and their meaning unpicked through shared discussion and research. Armed with these technical reading skills, children are enabled to read at greater depth, tapping into a limitless information source, thus developing a lifelong academic skill. Alexander and Jarman (2018) found children who then voluntarily choose to read science books described experiencing awe and wonder. Who would not want that for the children they teach?

Intuitively, we know that children are drawn to books that they either feel emotionally attached to or where the topic sparks their interest (Johnson and Giorgis, 2002). It may involve a cover-to-cover read, or an equally valid dip in and out to retrieve facts and information. Obviously, books are not the only source of information; answers can also be found online. Providing pupils with safe weblinks to use during class, or to explore at home, if they show an interest may encourage pupils to find out more for themselves. Museums (for example, the Smithsonian National Museum, the Natural History Museum), television channel sites (for example, the Discovery Channel) and specific websites for children's learning (for example, Enchanted Learning), have a wealth of scientific information there for children willing to engage and read the material on offer.

For science teachers, modelling good reading behaviour is of paramount importance. If we do not have an answer to a question, reaching for an encyclopaedia demonstrates that books are useful. In quiet reading time, the benefits of the teacher reading their book too have been well documented (Widdowson et al., 2006; Wheldall and Entwistle, 1988; Bandura, 1977). Maybe it is time to think about our choice of reading material, pick up a factual science book and expand our own scientific knowledge at the same time.

Case study: primary science – exploring lifecycles in stories and in real life

A Year 2 class focused on the lifecycles of animals and plants during the summer term for their science topic. The teacher, Sarah, led an initial discussion with the class to find out their understanding of animals' lifecycles, using Eric Carle's story *The Very Hungry Caterpillar* as a stimulus. In the story, the caterpillar gets fatter and fatter by eating a variety of treats, including lollipops and slices of Swiss cheese! It eventually builds its cocoon and metamorphoses into a butterfly.

This story was a familiar favourite for the class, with some children knowing every page by heart! Sarah wanted to develop the children's critical thinking skills in science lessons. After the class had read the story, she asked them: 'Which parts of this story do you think really happen to a caterpillar?' and: 'Are there any parts in this story which might have been made up?' To support them with this task, Sarah introduced the children to a range of non-fiction books on the theme of animals' lifecycles. Studying and discussing facts from these books helped the children to develop their knowledge and understanding of the processes involved in lifecycles. Sarah also used this activity to stimulate a discussion about the differences between fiction and factual books (for example, use of illustrations compared to photographs, and continuous prose compared to text boxes and diagrams).

For the next stage in the lifecycles topic, Sarah introduced the children to some new members of the class – five caterpillars! The caterpillars lived in their own 'house' (an enclosed cylindrical net), and the children investigated the types of food caterpillars preferred. Aligning with *The Very Hungry Caterpillar* story, the class put a lollipop and a slice of Swiss cheese into the caterpillar house, as well as fresh leaves. The children carefully noted that not only did the caterpillars prefer the leaves, but also made observations of how the caterpillars fed on the leaves, being introduced to the term 'mandibles'.

The process of metamorphosis was also observed, as the children saw the caterpillars building their cocoons, and finally witnessed the emergence of the butterflies. When observing the brown butterflies fluttering around, one child exclaimed: 'They don't look like the real one!' When Sarah asked what he meant, he picked up *The Very Hungry Caterpillar* book and showed her the beautiful multicoloured butterfly on the final page. 'Those ones are brown!' Fortunately, another child stepped in and showed him photographs of many different species of butterflies in the non-fiction books displayed in the classroom.

Later in the term, the class used another book by Eric Carle, *The Tiny Seed*, to initiate their scientific explorations into the topic of plant lifecycles. Sarah's discussion of the story with the class was a useful diagnostic assessment of the children's understanding and familiarity of plant lifecycles. The children explained what they thought a seed would need to help it to germinate, and then what they thought a plant would need for it to grow well, after germination. Again, factual books which focused on plant lifecycles were used to develop knowledge and understanding further.

Towards the end of term, ideas linked to biology were taken further using the book *James' Giant Bugs* (Elcomb, 2018), which is inspired by Roald Dahl's story *James and the Giant Peach*. The children were fascinated by the instructions in this book, including those that helped them to build their own bug hotels and construct ant farms. The colourful layout and fascinating facts about minibeasts meant that the class copies of this book were well-worn by the end of the topic!

Curriculum links

English	Science
Key Stage 1, Reading:	**Year 2, Animals, including humans:**
• to be introduced to non-fiction books that are structured in a variety of different ways;	• to notice that animals have offspring that will grow into adults; • to describe how animals obtain their food from plants and other animals, using the idea of a food chain, and identify and name different sources of food.

(Continued)

(Continued)

English	Science
• explain and discuss their understanding of books.	Year 2, Plants: • to observe and describe how seeds and bulbs grow into mature plants; • to find out how plants need water, light and a suitable temperature to grow and stay healthy.

Activity: children's classic literature – *The Iron Man* by Ted Hughes

The Iron Man tells the story of a gigantic metal robot who mysteriously appears, and is discovered by Hogarth, a young boy. The Iron Man devours farm machinery, until the farmers retaliate. Hogarth agrees to trap the monster, but the Iron Man escapes. Finally, Hogarth suggests that the monster should be allowed to feed in the scrap metal yard.

In the story, the Iron Man begins to devour all of the farmers' metal machinery before Hogarth suggests moving him to the scrap metal yard. The children could assist the Iron Man in identifying which metals are the 'most magnetic' and thus the most delicious metals to munch. They could then consider which metals would be the least scrumptious.

Hogarth thinks of ways to prevent the Iron Man from consuming the metal. The children could invent a machine based on magnetic properties which could thwart the Iron Man from consuming the farm equipment.

Consider the resources required in order to successfully conduct investigations linked to the National Curriculum objectives for magnetism.

Curriculum links

Science

Year 3, Forces and magnets

- observe how magnets attract or repel each other and attract some materials and not others;
- compare and group together a variety of everyday materials on the basis of whether they are attracted to a magnet, and identify some magnetic materials.

The language of mathematics

As well as developing opportunities from fiction and non-fiction texts in mathematics as outlined above for STEM subjects generally, this section looks at some of the particular challenges involved in the language of mathematics.

> 'Bitzer,' said Thomas Gradgrind. 'Your definition of a horse.'
>
> 'Quadruped. Graminivorous. Forty teeth, namely, twenty four grinders, four eye-teeth, and twelve incisive. Sheds coat in the spring; in marshy countries sheds hoof too. Hoofs hard, but requiring to be shod with iron. Age known by marks in mouth.' Thus (and much more) Bitzer.
>
> 'Now girl number twenty,' said Mr Gradgrind. 'You know what a horse is.'
>
> Charles Dickens, *Hard Times*, 1854

You can hear similar exchanges today. For example, in a Year 6 class where the pupils were revising 2-D shapes, they displayed adeptness at spelling 'parallelogram' and in reciting a definition ('two pairs of opposite sides that are parallel'), but struggled with the idea that a square could be a parallelogram. The aim of this chapter is to try to explain why this happens and to highlight the importance of talk and discussion to support reading and understanding in mathematics. Shuard and Rothery (1984) identified different types of mathematical words used in schools:

- technical vocabulary (words which are primarily mathematical like 'polygon' or 'divisor');

- lexical vocabulary (words which have a similar meaning in mathematics as in everyday English such as 'multiple' or 'remainder');

- everyday vocabulary (where words might have an overlapping meaning but a particular sense in a mathematical context such as 'point' or 'difference').

Almost all of the language used in mathematics lessons in primary schools has a particular sense or meaning which is determined by the context in which it is used. Sometimes this even varies between mathematics lessons, such as talking about difference or a (decimal) point in number and differences between shapes or a point in geometry. One way of developing mathematics teaching in primary schools is therefore to focus on such language and to use this perspective about talk and interaction as a means to support children's learning. Mathematical language is mentioned seventeen times in the Key Stages 1 and 2 programmes of study for mathematics, highlighting its importance in effective teaching.

Research focus: classroom talk

We know a lot about talk in classrooms (see, for example, Mercer and Dawes, 2014) where there are distinct patterns related to particular teaching objectives. Wood and Wood's (1988) research demonstrated that direct questions can be inhibiting, particularly for primary pupils, as children try to guess what the teacher wants as the reply, rather than make sense of the question. The dominant pattern of whole-class talk takes the form of a direct question from the teacher followed by a brief answer from a pupil, with a short evaluative follow-up statement from the teacher. This pattern can be effective, particularly when the objectives are to check for knowledge or information. However, if the objectives of a lesson are to promote pupil discussion and allow them to show or develop their thinking and reasoning, research suggests that direct questioning by the teacher can be counter-productive. This is particularly crucial in mathematics where the value of pupil talk is recognised as essential for developing understanding and making connections between mathematical ideas and mathematical skills and procedures (Raiker, 2002).

Case study: mathematical language

Nicole teaches Year 3 and used this 'odd one out' task (Higgins *et al.*, 2000) to elicit mathematical language from the children in her class.

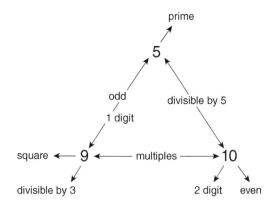

Figure 5.1   Odd one out task in maths (Higgins et al., 2000)

She presented the three numbers – 5, 9 and 10 – to the children; she asked them to find an odd one out and to give a reason why. The children quickly realised that there were lots of possible answers. She noticed that they did not always use the language she had been teaching such as 'multiples' or 'two-digit', but would say 'in the three times table' or 'has two numbers in it'. Choosing different combinations of three numbers (including those with two and three digits) let her explore the vocabulary the children were confident to use. She asked them to design their own 'odd one out' tasks in pairs and to set challenges for each other in finding all of the possible 'odd ones out' so that they could practise reading and writing this vocabulary. Nicole adapted the 'odd one out' task for work in shape and fractions later in the year.

Curriculum links

Mathematics

Year 3

- recognise the place value of each digit in a three-digit number;
- use multiples of 2, 3, 4, 5, 8, 10, 50 and 100;
- pupils should read and spell mathematical vocabulary correctly and confidently, using their growing word-reading knowledge and their knowledge of spelling.

Much of what happens in classrooms is not explicit and children interpret what is expected by unwritten rules and unspoken instructions. These linguistic or 'meta-discursive' (Kieran *et al.*, 2003) rules regulate how mathematics classrooms operate and profoundly influence both teachers and pupils. An example might be the way in which children interpret word problems in mathematics lessons. They know that such problems are typical in mathematics lessons and are used so that they can practise number operations. As a result, they pay little attention to whether or not the answer makes sense in the context of the problem and just do the sum by adding, subtracting or multiplying the numbers.

Teaching mathematics is particularly difficult because of the challenges that language poses (Schleppegrell, 2007). This is not just vocabulary. Mathematical discourse tends to use lots of nouns where the relationship between these is complex, so you need to understand the precise meanings of particular conjunctions and the implicit logical relationships that link words. For example, take this Year 6 problem:

The centre of a square has co-ordinates (3, 1) and one vertex at (−1, 5).

What are the co-ordinates of its other three vertices?

The language is highly compressed – a series of nouns (centre, co-ordinates, square, vertex) with a complex set of relationships which is partly determined by the concepts they embody, but also requires application of these concepts to solve the problem. No wonder some children struggle to decode the meaning!

This makes it particularly important that pupils do not just listen, but have opportunities to use mathematical language themselves such as in collaborative activities and in investigations and puzzles. This also gives you the chance as a teacher to assess and evaluate their understanding of not only the vocabulary, but also the mathematical understanding that they show (Higgins, 2003).

Activity: identifying confusing vocabulary in mathematics

Review the mathematics vocabulary for the year group you are next teaching. Which words are technical? Which are lexical? Which are everyday words used in a particular context? Where and how might misunderstanding arise?

For example 'difference' is lexical vocabulary which young children will probably have come across. It has a particular sense when teaching subtraction. If you set a problem such as 'Find the difference between 9 and 16,' you are not expecting the answer: 'Nine is an odd number and sixteen is even,' though this would literally be correct. What you want them to do is make a quantitative comparison and subtract 9 from 16.

Curriculum link

Numeracy and mathematics

5.1 Teachers should use every relevant subject to develop pupils' mathematical fluency. Confidence in numeracy and other mathematical skills is a precondition of success across the national curriculum.

Learning outcomes review

In this chapter you have learned about the importance and potential of the STEM curriculum for reading. This is both the contribution that STEM can make to reading and the importance of reading for STEM subjects. You have had the opportunity to see some practical examples of how reading can be integrated with science, technology and mathematics and the central role of reading in these activities. This has given you the opportunity to develop your knowledge about reading and its vital role in the wider curriculum in primary schools.

Conclusion

In this chapter we have considered how STEM and reading can be intricately and purposefully woven together, leading to learning benefits for children both within reading and also across the curriculum. When you are next planning a cross-curricular English topic, remember not to jump automatically to history, geography or art, but instead, try putting science, technology or mathematics at the top of the list! Not only will this develop children's subject knowledge, but it should also promote engagement and enjoyment through reading.

References

Alexander, J. and Jarman, R. (2018) The pleasures of reading non-fiction, *Literacy*, 52(2): 78–85.

Allington, R. (1994) The schools we have; the schools we need. *The Reading Teacher*, 48, 14–29.

Bandura, A. (1977) *Social Learning Theory*. Englewood Cliffs, NJ: Prentice-Hall.

Bortnem, G.M. (2011) Teacher use of interactive read alouds using nonfiction in early childhood classrooms. *Journal of College Teaching and Learning* (TLC), 5(12).

Bryce, N. (2011) Meeting the reading challenges of science textbooks in the primary grades. *The Reading Teacher*, 64(7): 474–85.

Camp, D. (2000) It takes two: teaching with twin texts of fact and fiction. *The Reading Teacher*, 53(5): 400–8.

Carle, E. (1994) *The Very Hungry Caterpillar*. London: Puffin.

Carle, E. (1997) *The Tiny Seed*. London: Puffin.

Cervetti, G.N., Barber, J., Dorph, R., Pearson, P.D. and Goldschmidt, P.G. (2012) The impact of an integrated approach to science and literacy in elementary school classrooms. *Journal of Research in Science Teaching*, 49(5): 631–58.

Cervetti, G.N., Wright, T.S. and Hwang, H. (2016) Conceptual coherence, comprehension, and vocabulary acquisition: a knowledge effect? *Reading and Writing*, 29(4): 761.

DfE (2011) *Teachers' Standards in England from September 2012*. London: DfE.

Dreher, M.J. and Kletzien, S.B. (2015) *Teaching Informational Text in K-3 Classrooms: Best Practices to Help Children Read, Write, and Learn from Nonfiction*. New York: Guilford.

Duke, N.K., Pearson, P.D., Strachan, S.L. and Bilman, A.K. (2011) Effective practices for developing reading comprehension, in A.E. Farstrup and S.J. Samuels (eds), *What Research has to Say about Reading Instruction* (4th edn). Newark, DE: International Reading Association, pp51–93.

Elcomb, B. (2018) *James' Giant Bugs*. London: Puffin.

Higgins, S. (2003) Parlez-vous mathematics? in I. Thompson (ed.), *Enhancing Primary Mathematics Teaching and Learning*. Buckingham: Open University Press.

Higgins, S.E., Baumfield, V. and Leat, D. (2000) *Thinking Through Primary Teaching*. Cambridge: Chris Kington.

Hoffman, J.L., Collins, M.F. and Schickedanz, J.A. (2015) Instructional challenges in developing young children's science concepts. *The Reading Teacher*, 68(5): 363–72.

Johnson, N. and Giorgis, C. (2002) Children's books: pleasure reading. *The Reading Teacher*, 55(8): 780–8.

Kieran, C., Forman, E. and Sfard, A. (2003) *Learning Discourse: Discursive Approaches to Research in Mathematics Education*. Dordrech: Kluwer.

Marra, G.R. (2014) Vocabulary growth using nonfiction literature and dialogic discussions in preschool classrooms. Doctoral dissertation, University of South Dakota.

Mercer, N. and Dawes, L. (2014) The study of talk between teachers and students, from the 1970s until the 2010s. *Oxford Review of Education*, 40(4): 430–45.

Moss, B. and Hendershot, J. (2002) Exploring sixth graders' selection of nonfiction trade books. *The Reading Teacher*, 56(1): 6–17.

Nagy, W. and Townsend, D. (2012) Words as tools: learning academic vocabulary as language acquisition. *Reading Research Quarterly*, 47(1): 91–108.

Norvell, G. (1950) *The Reading Interests of Young People*. East Lansing: Michigan State University Press

Palincsar, A.S. and Magnusson, S.J. (2001) The interplay of first-hand and second-hand investigations to model and support the development of scientific knowledge and reasoning, in S.M. Carver and D. Klahr (eds), *Cognition and Instruction: Twenty-Five Years of Progress*. New York: Psychology Press, pp151–93.

Pearson, P.D., Moje, E. and Greenleaf, C. (2010) Literacy and science: each in the service of the other. *Science*, 328(5977): 459–63.

Raiker, A. (2002) Spoken language and mathematics. *Cambridge Journal of Education*, 32(1): 45–60.

Schleppegrell, M.J. (2007) The linguistic challenges of mathematics teaching and learning: a research review. *Reading and Writing Quarterly*, 23(2): 139–59.

Shuard, H. and Rothery, A. (1984) *Children Reading Mathematics*. London: John Murray.

Snow, C.E. (2002) *Reading for Understanding: Toward an R&D Program in Reading Comprehension*. Santa Monica: RAND.

Wheldall, K. and Entwistle, J. (1988) Back in the USSR: the effect of teacher modelling of silent reading on pupils' reading behaviour in the primary school classroom. *Educational Psychology*, 8(1–2): 51–66.

Widdowson, D., Dixon, R. and Moore, D. (2006) The effects of teacher modelling of silent reading on students' engagement during sustained silent reading. *Educational Psychology*, 16(2): 171–80.

Wood, D. and Wood, H. (1988) Questioning versus student initiative, in J.T. Dillon (ed.), *Questioning and Discussion: A Multidisciplinary* Study. Norwood NJ: Ablex, pp280–305.

6 Developing a Love of Language for Performance through Poetry and Drama

Christina Castling and Charlotte Wright

A word is dead

When it is said,

    Some say.

I say it just

Begins to live

    That day.

'A Word is Dead', Emily Dickinson

Learning outcomes

By reading this chapter you will have considered:

- why active exploration of the spoken word should be an important part of classroom work;
- how you can build your confidence in helping your pupils to explore the spoken word through poetry and drama;
- how poetry and drama can provide opportunities to learn about language through play with words, voices and audiences;
- ways to create a safe and affirmative classroom where children feel happy to perform.

Teachers' Standards

3. Demonstrate good subject and curriculum knowledge:

- demonstrate an understanding of and take responsibility for promoting high standards of literacy, articulacy and the correct use of standard English.

4. Plan and teach well-structured lessons:

- promote a love of learning and children's intellectual curiosity;
- contribute to the design and provision of an engaging curriculum.

7. Manage behaviour effectively to ensure a good and safe working environment:

- manage classes effectively, using approaches which are appropriate to pupils' needs in order to involve and motivate them.

Curriculum link: spoken language

Years 1 to 6:

- use spoken language to develop understanding through speculating, hypothesising, imagining and exploring ideas;
- speak audibly and fluently with an increasing command of Standard English;
- participate in discussions, presentations, performances, roleplay/improvisations and debates;
- gain, maintain and monitor the interest of the listener(s);
- select and use appropriate registers for effective communication.

Introduction

You don't have to spend long in a primary school playground to spot the joy that children find in the spoken word. Whether it's well-rehearsed jeers at the opposing football team, chants about who fancies who, or imagined scenarios enacted among friends, children relish countless informal opportunities to entertain themselves with language in their independent play. This joy can be found within classrooms too, as these are exuberant places by their nature, full of lively talk and informal playacting. The particular kind of excitement children find in gathering words and 'performing' them in different ways suggests that poetry and drama – forms which are often by their nature performative – should be an easy fit in our lessons. As Emily Dickinson reminds us in the poem above, words spring into life as soon as they are spoken. Yet sometimes teachers hesitate when considering whether to include work on the spoken word, particularly in relation to poetry and drama.

In this chapter, we will address the importance of developing pupils' appreciation of the spoken word and explore practical ways of fostering a love of language-out-loud, with a view to making oral performance part of school culture and everyday practice. Short activities, case studies and links to relevant research are included to broaden understanding, along with advice about how to ensure the classroom is a safe space for trying out different voices and different approaches.

The importance of developing skill in relation to spoken language is well established (Millard and Menzies, 2016), with language competence linked to educational attainment (Roulstone *et al.*, 2011) and a positive sense of self (Trickey and Topping, 2006; Ofsted, 2010). Patsy Rodenburg, a highly successful voice coach from the Guildhall School of Music and Drama, reminds us that in every individual is a life force, and that vocal presence is 'a universal quality that we all have but is [often] somehow flattened out of us' (Rodenburg, 2009, xiv). As primary teachers, we have the chance to help every pupil celebrate that life force and develop that presence through energising and energetic work with the spoken word. We will all want and need to make ourselves heard in our lives, and one important job of schooling is to get pupils to perceive themselves as creative speakers and performers worthy of attention. Before launching into practicalities, however, it is worth pausing to think about our own experiences, and to consider how these may have shaped our attitudes as teachers.

Activity

Take some time to revisit your personal experiences of exploring the spoken word at school.

- What memories do you have of participating in poetry and drama in the classroom as a child/teenager?
- What was positive about these experiences?
- What was negative about these experiences?
- Did any of the poetry or drama make it out of the school gates and into your home environment?
- Did you bring any poetry or drama from home into the classroom?
- What are the ways in which these early experiences have influenced your approach to poetry and drama as a teacher?

Sharing these questions and your answers with a colleague will provide opportunity for valuable deeper reflection.

Case study: trainee teachers' experiences of poetry

At the beginning of a university session about teaching poetry, primary trainee teachers were asked to name as many poems as they could, and then were asked about their memories of poetry at school. Straight away many thought of poems from GCSE poetry exam antholo-gies, which they had tried to learn by heart with varying degrees of success, and many

→

thought about the intensity of exam preparation with pages of notes copied from the board, a race through the contexts of the poems and set structures for responding relating to mark schemes. Nobody could remember performing poetry at secondary school and most had had their last encounters with poetry aged sixteen. Typical comments included:

- 'The teacher was very stressed about getting us through a lot of poems in a short amount of time.'

- 'There wasn't much room for me to say what I thought.'

- 'I never really understood what we were learning them *for.*'

- 'I kept quiet when I didn't understand a poem.'

These responses indicate that some teachers may approach the idea of poetry and/or spoken word performance in the classroom with reservations, with the voices and messages from poems retained only as faint echoes rather than a vibrant choir.

The National Curriculum has included reference to both drama and poetry in its content since its first appearance in 1989, but research into teacher attitudes and perspectives shows some enduring patterns around issues of confidence, suggesting that poetry and drama can be sites of anxiety for both new and experienced teachers.

Research focus

Wright's (1999) research indicates that many students entering teacher training confess to feeling nervous or apprehensive about participating in drama in the classroom. Dickinson and Neelands (2012) offer an illustration of this anxiety when they share the concerns of Rachel, a Year 6 teacher, as 'an honest assessment of concerns' that teachers may harbour: 'I didn't know how certain children would react to a more active approach to learning. I was particularly worried about the kids who struggle with behaviour during normal lessons' (Dickinson and Neelands, 2012, p36).

Research into attitudes to the teaching of poetry shows that teacher apprehension often lies more with mastery of the subject matter than its delivery. Peter Benton conducted research into teachers' views about teaching poetry in the 1980s and 1990s (Benton, 1984, 1999) and discovered that a substantial number of teachers surveyed were worried about their own knowledge and teaching skill, even while expressing the view that poetry was important and valuable as part of an English education. While teachers found value in poetry as a means of developing children's awareness of the infinite possibilities of language; a way of discovering and exploring shared experience and feelings; and a vehicle for fun and cultural

$\longrightarrow$

understanding, there were also common concerns, some of which can be heard anew in the case study above. These included:

- A concern with children's own hostility towards poetry as unfamiliar or irrelevant

- A sense of pressure about providing and/or eliciting 'correct' interpretations

- A lack of confidence in relation to choosing, sharing and unpacking poetry

(Benton, 1984, pp325-6)

Establishing a supportive environment

Activity

Imagine that at the end of a full staff meeting, you're asked by the Head to stand up in front of your colleagues and read a short story aloud. You're expected to use funny voices for different characters, there are some words you have no idea how to pronounce and, after you've taken a deep breath and read the first few words, the Head interrupts you, saying: 'Come on, louder than that.'

- Jot down three words to describe how you might feel.
- Have you experienced situations in which children have been put in a similar position? How might they feel?
- When a child in your class is reading aloud, how do you want them to feel? And what could you consciously do as a teacher to make them feel this way?

Whether the prospect of planning to use poetry and drama in your classroom elicits a moment of hesitation or a yelp of delight, every teacher can take simple steps to establish clear parameters which will help make spoken word work in the classroom feel less daunting for all.

- *Fix the expectations*: set aside time to establish and agree upon some basic rules, and keep these permanently visible. For example:
  - give whoever is speaking your full attention;
  - remember that all of us find performing challenging at times: give encouragement rather than criticism;
  - give a huge round of applause at the end of any sharing or performance;
  - look out for what works well and what would make it even better.

- *Go from group to individual*: hearing your voice ring out in a big space is less frightening if you have first heard it alongside the voices of others. Start with full class or group work to familiarise a performance environment.

- *Demonstrate with gusto*: if you are expecting your class to be brave and speak in new ways, join them. Be prepared to show when you are stepping out of your comfort zone and this will give your children permission to do the same, modelling boldness in creative decisions.

- *Practise peer encouragement*: after any performance, give the children opportunities to celebrate each other's work, ensuring that criticism is kindly given. This will hone their skills as both performers and audience members. Provide sentence stems for the children to use to get this process going if you think your class needs them, such as 'I really liked the way you …' or 'It was very effective when you …'.

- *Be specific with praise*: rather than a vague 'That was great!', build confidence and subject knowledge by highlighting distinct performance skills as they are demonstrated:

  o Wow, James, your *enunciation* was superb then. You spoke every word really clearly.

  o Fantastic *projection* Rafiq. I could hear everything you said.

  o Your *actions* and *gestures* really helped me understand what you were saying. Well done, Ella-May.

  o Wonderful *pace* Jenny. You spoke slowly enough for me to catch every word.

- *Plan small and large opportunities to perform*: whether to each other, the rest of the Key Stage, the whole school or an invited audience of parents/carers, the chance to share work with a new audience can give a useful focus for any performance work. Remember that the 'scarier' the audience feels, the more rehearsal is needed and, for particularly nervous children, additional support may need to be put in place (for example, working with a partner or recording words in advance).

Bridges in and out of the world of the classroom

Often, resources for projects to improve oral skills in the classroom focus on formal register via discussion, analysis and reasoning (e.g. Dawes, 2011). Yet when we use poetry and drama to learn about the spoken word, the focus does not have to be on each child becoming a scholarly debater or renouncing the identity they already have as a speaker in the home or playground. Poetry and drama can be used for a different function, to build crossing points between informal and formal activity, creating bridges in and out of the world of the classroom.

As teachers, it is important that we generate enthusiasm for language and help our pupils enjoy creative play with voice and meaning. The following three principles can help shape a vibrant approach to using drama and poetry:

- embrace play and silliness;
- explore through experience;
- notice and bend the rules.

Embrace play and silliness

Bringing the spoken word into the classroom doesn't have to mean plunging into intense recitals showcasing the loudest pupils' elocution and star quality. From Early Years to Year 6, children can be enticed into more relaxed and familiar kinds of playfulness with speech. In researching young children's attitudes to work and play, Goodhall and Atkinson (2019) discovered that 'even very young children can conceptualize and articulate dimensions of "play" and "work"', but if teachers split the two apart rather than presenting them as a continuum, it can have a potentially negative impact on children's engagement, their well-being and their sense of ownership of their experiences (Goodhall and Atkinson, 2019, p1703). Thus, we would do well to see play-based learning as rich with possibility rather than as threatening disorder. And, of course, the classroom should be somewhere that is fun for us too!

Jokes and riddles are an excellent starting point in that they represent tiny acts of performance involving attention to language, narrative or audience engagement in question and answer, as well as encouraging attentive listening. As mini-scripts, they can be taught at speed, with emphasis on the importance of the sequence and the pause and, once learned, children readily accept the challenge to carry them out of the classroom context to use them with wider audiences. Consider how the humble knock-knock joke offers an instant kind of linguistic satisfaction:

> *Knock knock.*
> *Who's there?*
> *Joe.*
> *Joe who?*
> *Only Joe King …*

Most classes will need very little encouragement to share known versions, and engage in word play in creating their own logical or surreal adaptations.

Activity

See how quickly you yourself can conjure an ending to the following examples, using names:

> *Knock Knock.*
> *Who's there?*
> *Anita / Olive / Luke / Isabel / Mikey*

Now take a moment to consider what tactics you used to try to fashion a punchline. Did you come up with anything like the following endings?

- *Anita use the bathroom so open the door!*
- *Olive here so let me in!*
- *Luke through the keyhole and you will see!*
- *Isabel not working?*
- *Mikey is stuck in the lock!*

You may well have opted for alliteration, homophones, rhyme or half-rhyme, or even idiom. Would anyone be able to understand your punchline? Or would the joke have particular resonance for a specific group of friends or family? A class discussion with older students about how far the joke might be able to 'travel' might highlight how the guessing or creation of punchlines requires a shared knowledge of the social world.

You might also model the sharing of riddles, drawing attention to the micro-tactics a good storyteller might deploy to keep the attention of their audience.

1. Read the following riddles out loud so that your class can try to guess the answers:

   This mother comes from a family of eight,
   Supports her children in spite of their weight.
   She turns around without being called,
   And has held you since the time you crawled. (Earth)

   I go up and I go down,
   Towards the sky and towards the ground.
   I'm present and past tense too
   Come join me for a ride – but you'll need a friend with you. (Seesaw)

2. Now read them again, this time in an exaggerated monotone, and ask the class to give you pointers as to how to bring them to life. You could offer the following prompts if the class were stuck: 'speed', 'pause', 'emphasis', 'volume', 'facial expression', or 'action'.
3. Retell the riddles using the children's pointers until they are happy with your performance, and remind them that audience feedback can lead to more successful performances.

Riddles might also function as ways to play with spoken language, sound and sequence. Work with riddles can support the growth of phonological awareness – a sensitivity to the sound structure of words, from the tiny units of phonemes, through onset-rime into syllables, and on into rhyme – alongside consideration of meaning.

Research focus

This kind of activity also has value in that it highlights the prosodic aspects of texts: that is, patterns of stress, intonation, tone and rhythm – the music of the spoken word. Studies indicate that awareness of prosody plays a significant role in how young children process both written and spoken language (Herman, 1985; Dowhower, 1991). Prosodic knowledge has a role in facilitating reading comprehension (Kuhn and Stahl, 2000; Cypert and Petro, 2019) and can also be linked to writing skill: Chafe (1988) suggests that proficient writers monitor, listen to and nurture an inner voice of prosody as they write.

In a specific example of linking theory to practice, Ness (2009) recounts using guided prosodic practice in relation to humorous texts in the form of choral and echo readings. She describes preparing a class for a 'Comedy Hour', in which pupils performed rehearsed readings for classmates or visitors, and was able to identify the gains children made in reading fluency and confidence when prosody was a focus.

Prosodic play with jokes and riddles can thus act as a support with wider literacy development, as well as helping children to perceive themselves as successful speakers and entertainers. Such work could be brought back into play later in the crafting of more formal written and spoken persuasive texts, as humour and wordplay can have an important place in winning over readers and listeners.

Explore through experience

When taking part in drama, children engage in what Winston (2004, p6) describes as 'an imaginative act that in many ways reflects the transformative powers of magic'. This 'magic' enables spaces, people and objects to become wholly different from what they are in reality and the opportunity to explore experiences contained within words on a page presents itself. Children who may never see the Lake District daffodils of William Wordsworth's 'I Wandered Lonely as a Cloud' can dance among them in the school hall. Those who are unlikely to go on safari can encounter William Blake's 'Tyger' prowling around the playground. While a fear of losing classroom control can easily lead to a decision to stay behind a desk, that is to lose the immense potential for deeper understanding and engagement that drama affords. Getting the spoken word up on its feet breathes life into its meaning and can captivate the most reluctant of readers.

Activity: 'Lone Dog' by Irene McLeod

Irene McLeod's three-stanza poem about a wild dog who sneers at a life of comfort and company, overflows with opportunities for dramatic exploration. The barrage of sparse description and the fast-paced flow of verbs almost beg to be acted out. Complicated drama exercises are not necessary; any activities that get the class exploring the poem physically and/or vocally will lead to a more nuanced and sophisticated understanding of the text. Using a staple classroom drama exercise as a starting point, let's consider ways of approaching 'Lone Dog' experientially:

- *Still images (tableaux)*: before reading the poem, split the class into small groups and allocate a different couplet to each. After each group has created a still image to represent the words, share these and discuss what can be seen. Compare these observations with the couplets.
- *Enact the poem*: very simply, act out the words. Bring short sections of the poem to life through movement. For example, what would 'a tough dog, hunting on my own' or 'a lap dog, licking dirty feet' look like?
- *Five-word list*: in pairs or small groups, circle five important words from the poem (for example, mad, moon, kick, wild, quest) and practise speaking these aloud, considering volume, tone and emotion. Hear these five-word lists one after the other and discuss prominent words and themes.
- *Soundscape*: with one person reading extracts from the poem aloud, the rest of the group create an accompanying soundscape – for example, the footfall of 'dogs running by my side' and the 'wide wind' howling. Listening to this with eyes closed can heighten the listening experience.
- *Your choice*: give the class freedom to present the poem however they choose and, after sharing the performances, discuss what motivated the creative decisions. The following prompts may be useful before they take fifteen to twenty minutes to plan and rehearse.

    o   Who is going to say which words/lines of the poem?
    o   How will you act out specific parts of the poem?
    o   How could you use sounds to create atmosphere?

Activity extension: if you were to share one of the following poems with your class, consider how you might use and adapt some of the techniques explored above:

- 'Joy at the Sound' by Roger McGough;
- 'Emma Hackett's Newsbook' by Allan Ahlberg;
- 'My Many Coloured Days' by Dr Seuss.

Case study: bringing 'The Cataract of Lodore' to life.

The Year 5 class in a Durham city primary school were preparing to share Robert Southey's 'The Cataract of Lodore' in an assembly and enlisted the help of a drama facilitator. During a one-hour workshop, the children took part in a series of fast-paced activities designed to improve performance skills and deepen understanding of the poem.

→

Using lines from the text as a vocal warm-up, the class began by reciting: 'Confounding, astounding,/Dizzying and deafening the ear with its sound' in a variety of different ways, including quickly, quietly, happily and deeply. They were then split into five groups, each with a different stanza. They were given minutes to learn the lines, then each group was asked to deliver their section in a specific way:

- as if telling a secret;

- as if in a big rush;

- with everyone talking over each other;

- as one voice, altogether;

- as if fighting to be heard.

These tasks enabled the children to engage with the text experientially, their actions and voices mimicking the water's movement – for example, delivering 'hurrying and skurrying,/And thundering and floundering' as if in a rush and speaking 'flushing and brushing and gushing', as if fighting to be heard.

By the end of the session, not only was the poem ready for a whole-class performance, but the children also had a fresh grasp of how the language was crafted by the poet to achieve his artistic aims.

Notice and bend the rules

We can also use close attention to the spoken word to explore instances of language 'rules' being flexed or subverted as a form of playing. The way that poetic and drama texts are laid out puts open air around words, drawing greater attention to their arrangement: we can slip the net of prose into liberating white space on the page.

Poetry in particular is often about the bringing together of the familiar and the strange, and we can use everyday examples to get children to hold language up to the light. Metaphor and simile work by overlaying one image with an illuminating other, and can be pulled from pop songs and advertising jingles for unpacking. How is the imagery in Pharrell Williams' famous call to 'clap your hands if you feel like a room without a roof' working to illustrate a particular emotion, for example? Instances of oxymoron from commonplace speech can also intrigue when scrutinised. What are the meanings of the following illogical pairings, and how might they have come into use?

bitter sweet
lead balloon
clearly misunderstood

old news
dull roar
only choice

The horizons of expression can also be explored, for example in those instances where words themselves aren't quite enough; children (and indeed adults) of all ages enjoy the slide into chocolatey bliss of the nocturnal cake thief in Michael Rosen's *Chocolate Cake,* where language itself reaches its limits:

A whole slice this time,
into the mouth.
Oh the icing on top
and the icing in the middle
ohhhhhh oooo mmmmmm…

At a broader textual level, the dramatic monologue in poetic form gives pupils the chance to encounter and (re)invent distinctive voices in creative ways. Roald Dahl's games with fairy tales in *Revolting Rhymes* offer humorous templates for using poetry or monologue to subvert familiar story structures. Older readers might enjoy the ingenuity in extracts from Carol Ann Duffy's *Mrs Midas*, or *Elvis' Twin Sister.*

One route into poetic monologue which foregrounds the performative elements of the spoken word is to take familiar spoken text types and ruffle their edges. Popular examples might include the word play with place names in Michael Rosen's 'Here Are the Football Results':

Here are the football results:
League Division Fun
Manchester United won, Manchester City lost.
Crystal Palace 2, Buckingham Palace 1
Millwall Leeds nowhere
Wolves 8. A cheese roll and had a cup of tea 2
Newcastle's Heaven Sunderland's a very nice place 2
Ipswhich one? You tell me.

or Adrian Henri's interruption of Wordsworth with the clamorous voice of the advertisement:

'The New, Fast, Automatic Daffodils'
(New variation on Wordsworth's 'Daffodils')

I wandered lonely as
THE NEW, FAST DAFFODIL
FULLY AUTOMATIC

that floats on high o'er vales and hills
The Daffodil is generously dimensioned to accommodate four adult passengers
10,000 saw I at a glance
Nodding their new anatomically shaped heads in sprightly dance
Beside the lake beneath the trees
– in three bright modern colours
red, blue and pigskin
The Daffodil de luxe is equipped with a host of useful accessories …

Case study: hijacking familiar forms

Primary pupils Toby and Jack (working collaboratively in a joint Year 4 and Year 6 project) produced these sentences and phrases when asked what these spoken texts might sound like:

A TV weather report:

- *And today the weather is very wet down in the South of England …*

- *A light breeze is sweeping through England. Storm Bruce is on its way, so I recommend you stay inside …*

Instructions from the dentist:

- *Please sit on the chair. Open wide – I won't bite! Have your teeth been hurting recently?*

- *Please sit back on the seat. How often do you brush your teeth? It's fine … we're just going to do a little operation …*

A TV talent show voiceover:

- *Next up, we have Donald about to sing 'Let It Go!' The audience is going wild for him!*

- *The next act is performed by Alex.*

A librarian's instructions on how to use the library:

- *Do not run or shout. You can take a book out but after a while you have to bring it back. Please take care of the books and don't damage them.*

- *Please be very quiet. Don't rip the books. Please feel free to take any book you want.*

From these responses, you can start to hear the way that children carry other voices in their heads, both individually and in terms of patterns of content, vocabulary and sentence structure. After looking at the Rosen and Henri poems and being offered a list of spoken word texts, Toby and Jack

→

chose to try blending a weather report with a baking show voiceover. After listening to real examples of both, they enjoyed gathering common phrases to create and perform new hybrid texts:

A slight chance of icing sugar on high surfaces is expected,
with dough rising rapidly in the afternoon ...

Expect some milk flooding in the sink,
with temperatures feeling gradually cooler
when the fridge is opened ...

Sponge will sink southwards
during warm spells in the oven,
but cookies are not expected to last into the afternoon ...

Activity

Look at these examples of spoken word texts from the world outside the classroom. What activities could you devise to help children explore and imitate them, individually or collectively?

- Train platform announcement
- Film trailer
- Sports commentary
- Radio traffic report
- Fitness podcast.

Your class could then be encouraged to take ownership of each text by *recreating* them and performing them:

- as if spoken for a new audience (for example, a radio traffic report for deep sea divers);
- as if spoken on a new occasion (for example, a train platform announcement for the first ever hover-train);
- as if spoken with an unexpected emotion (for example, football commentary by the groundsman who had just finished perfecting every blade of grass on the pitch) ...

By embracing (1) play and silliness, (2) exploring through experience and (3) noticing and bending the rules, we can give the spoken word a more prominent place in the classroom. This kind of work doesn't mean we are promoting a lack of focus, a slackening of discipline or an excuse for hyperactivity. Instead, we should think about the benefits: play with drama and poetry can and should lead to vibrant lessons, where creative boundaries are explored and extended, and outcomes may remain unpredictable – all things that characterise a dynamic learning environment. By assigning time to listen to their voices, we will be giving children valuable opportunities to experience the spoken word in new ways, and shape new performative selves.

Learning outcomes review

Now that you have read this chapter, you should understand:

- why active exploration of the spoken word is important work in the classroom;
- how to build your confidence in helping your pupils to explore poetry and drama out loud;
- the opportunities that poetry and drama can provide in terms of learning about language through play with words, voices and audiences;
- how you can create a safe and affirmative classroom where children feel happy to perform.

Conclusion

Drama and poetry are versatile tools to help us bring language to life in the classroom and show our pupils how its power can be explored and enjoyed in a multitude of ways.

When we talk about language with our pupils, we need to help them see that we do not mean mere static words on a page, somebody else's texts to be rehearsed and approved, but a dynamic, living, breathing force, full of magic and opportunity. To engage an audience with the spoken word is to hold them in the spell of the moment, and the classroom is a space in which teacher as well as student can build up confidence in the skills of enchantment. Let's heed Emily Dickinson's poetic insight and get our children accomplished at exploring and performing their experiences and thoughts both in and beyond the classroom. For while silence has an important place in school, so too does the fun and empowerment that comes with playing with words out loud.

References

Benton, P. (1984) Teaching poetry: the rhetoric and the reality. *Oxford Review of Education*, 10(3): 319–27.

Benton, P. (1999) Unweaving the rainbow: poetry teaching in the secondary school 1. *Oxford Review of Education*, 25(4): 521–31.

Chafe, W. (1988) Punctuation and the prosody of written language. *Written Communication*, 5(4): 395–426.

Cypert, R. and Petro, M. (2019) Prosody instruction intervention as a means to improved reading comprehension. *Applied Cognitive Psychology*, 33(6): 1305.

Dawes, L. (2011) *Talking Points: Discussion Activities in the Primary Classroom*. Abingdon: Routledge.

Dickinson, R. and Neelands, J. (2012) *Improve Your Primary School Through Drama*. Abingdon: David Fulton.

Dowhower, S. (1991) Speaking of prosody: fluency's unattended bedfellow. *Theory Into Practice*, 30(3): 165–75.

Goodhall, N. and Atkinson, C. (2019) How do children distinguish between 'play' and 'work'? Conclusions from the literature. *Early Child Development and Care*, 189: 10.

Henri, A., Patten, B. and McGough, R. (2007) *The Mersey Sound*. London: Penguin Modern Classics.

Herman, P. (1985) The effect of repeated readings on reading rate, speech pauses and word recognition accuracy. *Reading Research Quarterly*, 20(5): 553–65.

Kuhn, M. and Stahl, S.A. (2000) *Fluency: A Review of Developmental and Remedial Practices*. Ann Arbor, MI: Center for the Improvement of Early Reading Achievement. National Institute of Child Health and Human.

Millard, W. and Menzies, L. (2016) *The State of Speaking in Our Schools*. London: Voice 21/ LKMco.

Ness, M. (2009) Laughing through re-readings: using joke books to build fluency. *Reading Teacher*, 62(8): 691–4.

Ofsted (2010) *Learning: Creative Approaches That Raise Standards*. Manchester: Ofsted, pp5, 19.

Rodenburg, P. (2009) *Presence: How to Use Positive Energy for Success in Every Situation*. London: Penguin.

Rosen, M. and McGough, R. (2015) *You Tell Me*. London: Frances Lincoln.

Rosen, M. and Waldron, K. (2018) *Chocolate Cake*. London: Penguin Random House.

Roulstone, S., Law, J., Rush., R., Clegg, J. and Peters, T. (2011) *Investigating the Role of Language in Children's Early Educational Outcomes*, Research Report DFE-RR134 (9).

Southey, R. (1995) *Cataract of Lodore*. New York: Smithmark.

Trickey, S. and Topping, K.J. (2006) Collaborative philosophical enquiry for school children: socioemotional effects at 11–12 years. *School Psychology International*, 27: 599–614.

Winston, J. (2004) *Drama and English at the Heart of the Curriculum: Primary and Middle Years.* London: David Fulton.

Wright, P. (1999) The thought of doing drama scares me to death. *Research in Drama Education*, 4(2): 227–37.

7 Building Diversity and Inclusion through Books

Diana Mann and Amanda Nuttall

Learning outcomes

By reading this chapter you will have considered:

- what some of the current issues related to teaching inclusivity and diversity are;
- how to audit available texts and choose high-quality inclusive books;
- how to make sure all children in your class are represented in the books we read;
- how to use inclusive books to challenge stereotypes and normalise difference.

Teachers' Standards

1. Set high expectations which inspire, motivate and challenge pupils:

- establish a safe and stimulating environment for pupils, rooted in mutual respect;
- set goals that stretch and challenge pupils of all backgrounds, abilities and dispositions;
- demonstrate consistently the positive attitudes, values and behaviour which are expected of pupils.

5. Adapt teaching to respond to the strengths and needs of all pupils:

- have a secure understanding of how a range of factors can inhibit pupils' ability to learn, and how best to overcome these;
- demonstrate an awareness of the physical, social and intellectual development of children, and know how to adapt teaching to support pupils' education at different stages of development;
- have a clear understanding of the needs of all pupils, including those with special educational needs; those of high ability; those with English as an additional language; those with disabilities; and be able to use and evaluate distinctive teaching approaches to engage and support them.

(Continued)

(Continued)

8. Fulfil wider professional responsibilities:

- develop effective professional relationships with colleagues, knowing how and when to draw on advice and specialist support;
- take responsibility for improving teaching through appropriate professional development, responding to advice and feedback from colleagues;
- communicate effectively with parents with regard to pupils' achievements and well-being.

Part 2 of Teachers' Standards: showing tolerance of and respect for the rights of others.

Curriculum links

The National Curriculum Statutory Guidance, Section 4, sets out principles for the inclusion of all pupils, with two main requirements:

- setting suitable challenges;
- responding to pupils' needs and overcoming potential barriers for individuals and groups of pupils.

(DfE, 2014)

Introduction

We all remember, as children, curling up somewhere quiet and getting lost in the pages of a good book. What was it that made us so engrossed? Partly escapism and the suspension of disbelief, but often it was about being able to see ourselves in the role of the main character or hero. Seeing ourselves represented in a book – fiction or non-fiction – opens up our social imaginary of what might be. But not everyone has this opportunity. What if, as a child, you cannot find books that you can relate to; you cannot find a hero to become; you cannot see a situation in a book which relates to a life like yours? Does this make you less likely to want to read a book and to want to escape into the pages of a book?

In the UK we have a rich diversity of population. Let's start by considering ethnicity: data from 2015 highlighted that 6.1 per cent of primary school teachers in England are from a non-white background, compared to 31.4 per cent of the pupils that they teach (Runnymede Trust/NASUWT, 2017). This suggests there is potentially a large gap in representation, where children from ethnic minority backgrounds may be less likely to see themselves represented in the ethnic make-up of their teachers over the course of their schooling. It is clear that this lack of representation is a real concern, but we need to be careful not to limit conversations about diversity in schools to ethnicity and associated cultures, neglecting the broad landscape of other aspects of diversity (Race, 2017). The structure, size and shape of the family have changed considerably in recent years, as have our understandings of gender and sexuality. Let's not forget [dis]ability – 15 per cent of school-aged children have some form of special educational need (DfE, 2019). Then there are further issues to consider related to socio-economic or 'class' status, religious belief and, of course, *intersectionality* (Crenshaw, 1989). Taking such factors into consideration can mean young people feel marginalised or disenfranchised in a number of different ways.

The books that we use in our classroom and our curriculum provide a window into our diversity practice. Many good-quality, inclusive books already exist, and many teachers are using these in their everyday practice. For example, Letterbox Library (www.letterboxlibrary.com/) specialises in supplying children's books which recognise diversity in all senses of the word, but these kinds of books need to be highlighted, celebrated and promoted – and we need more of them. In this chapter, we will consider some of the ways in which books could – and should – be used to promote diversity and inclusion. A central thread lies in building children's motivation to read, through providing texts where they can make connections and see realistic representations of themselves and their lives. As we will discuss, this means more than tokenistic representation, or using diverse books for teaching a specific 'topic' or addressing an 'issue'. A crucial starting point is taking time to consider what is at issue, and how you can develop knowledge and understanding of locally sensitive and contextual concerns in individual classrooms or schools.

Focusing on diversity

As teachers, it is important that we consider our own understandings in relation to the full scope of diversity, as well as acknowledging our own positionality and how this may affect our interpretation or response to diversity in its various guises. These can be difficult issues to talk about, not least because they are often rooted in normative social and cultural understandings related to identity. These kinds of messages are often subtle and nuanced, hidden in our everyday conversations, media messages and policy documents. It would be naive of us to consider, as teachers, that we do not play a key role in [unintentionally] reproducing existing social barriers and hierarchies. As Eaude (2020) points out, the formal curriculum (i.e. the National Curriculum and associated schemes of work) is only one dimension of children's curriculum experience. Perhaps more powerful is the 'hidden' (or subliminal) curriculum, where insidious messages about what it means to be black, or female, or lesbian, or disabled are key in shaping an individual's identity. For teachers, recognising this process and taking action to consider what stigmatising or stereotypical messages may be [re]produced in our curriculum materials is an important first step.

Children are not born with prejudice. It's something they acquire as they get older. Reeves and Kirk (2018) reflect on how, by the ages of 3 to 4, children are unashamed to express themselves freely and without prejudice. This coincides with children starting their formal education and it is often at this point they start to hear direct statements which fuel normative assumptions about gender, race and culture. This means that our curriculum in the EYFS and KS1 is highly influential in shaping children's perceptions. If, as teachers, we want to reduce stereotyping beliefs then we need to normalise difference. This means embedding diversity, and books provide a vital opportunity to share both explicit and implicit messages about difference.

Research focus: gender representation

Some might question whether books and characterisation – for example, those linked to gender stereotypes – can impact on children. They might not feel that reading about stereotypical characters in books would lead children to behave in certain ways or maybe even influence life and career choices. Research tends to state differently.

The *Drawing the Future* report (Education and Employers, 2018) discovered that by the age of seven children's aspirations appear to be shaped by gender-related stereotypes about who does certain jobs. When asked to draw a picture of the career they saw for themselves when they grow up, it was clear that boys tended to aspire towards traditionally male-dominated professions and girls to show a greater tendency towards nurturing and caring related roles. Forty-five per cent of the children based their choices on influences from things they had seen and read. Although this was predominantly film, television and media, it indicates that children are influenced by the portrayal of gender roles beyond people they know. If the characters they encounter in books reinforce gender stereotypes, then this potentially becomes embedded in their thinking and beliefs.

Singh (1998) stated that, overall, girls are portrayed less frequently than boys in children's books, noting that both genders are often shown in stereotypical roles. Ernst (1995) further identified that girls are commonly shown as characters who are 'sweet, naive, conforming, and dependent'. In contrast, male characters are far more independent and have characteristics such as strength, aggression and looking for adventure (cited in Mermelstein, 2018). Temple (1993) outlined how boy characters in books tend to have roles as adventurers and rescuers, while girl characters are more likely to have passive roles as mothers, sisters or princesses who need rescuing. Female characters tend to support the main male figure. Kramer (2001) supports this view and outlines how girl characters are regularly shown as more nurturing, taking on roles as mothers, nurses and helpers. Rudman (1995) goes further, describing that if there is a strong girl character initially, they 'soon relinquish their independence, or are *tamed*, by a male character or situation that occurs in their lives' (cited in Mermelstein, 2018). This type of characterisation can still be identified in children's books today and, if it is not addressed, will inevitably give children clear, but subtle messages about their roles in society.

→

Even books with animal characters tend towards gender stereotypes. As Chatfield highlights, 'males were more typically embodied as powerful, wild and potentially dangerous beasts such as dragons, bears and tigers, while females tended to anthropomorphise smaller and more vulnerable creatures such as birds, cats and insects' – or as a commentator put it, 'prey' (www.thersa.org/discover/publications-and-articles/rsa-blogs/2019/03/gender-books).

Activity

It has been recognised that, as teachers, we sometimes make assumptions or hold unconscious bias about the children and families we work with. It is important that we reflect on our actions and interactions within our classroom and school context. This cycle of critical reflection – or enquiry – can help us understand what is at issue and generate potential solutions (for an example from practice, see Nuttall and Doherty, 2014).

Start by describing your class – this could be a written description or a mind-map style exercise. What is the physical environment like? What is the make-up of your class? Think about gender, race, religion, class. What are the children's relationships like with each other? Try to be specific in this consideration and be careful that you don't make generalisations.

Now go back through your description and highlight any common themes. Are there any patterns in children's achievement? What about their engagement? Are there any issues in classroom dynamics? Are there any individuals or groups that you know less about compared to others?

This first part of the activity helps you to consider the diversity of your classroom. You might also be able to identify patterns that concern you – for example, finding that you know less about some of the EAL children in your class, or that there is a link between gender and ability grouping in English. Some of these patterns might alert you to unconscious bias in the way you respond to groups of children you work with. This can be a challenging reflection!

Now let's focus on your experiences of the reading curriculum and resources. Consider the books you use, or have used, with a class or group of children. Are all children and their families represented equally in these books? Might there be a relationship between children's engagement with reading and how they see themselves represented in the books they have access to? Do the books they read reflect their own life experiences? Can they make connections?

(Continued)

You might be able to identify some gaps in resources which could disenfranchise some children – especially minority groups. This is a good starting point for identifying any gaps that you may need to address in your choice of texts you will use in the future. As we will consider in the next section, it is essential for children's personal and social development that they see themselves represented authentically in text, as well as seeing varied representations of others.

Improving representation in books

It is crucial that children can 'see' themselves in the books and stories they read. For some of us this is our lived experience, but if we reflect on the books we loved as children, books in our libraries, schools and on our home bookshelves, we may recognise that books commonly distort the world view towards one that is predominantly white and middle class. Rudine Sims Bishop (1990) writes about books being windows, mirrors or sliding doors. 'Windows' enable children to gain a glimpse into another world, maybe a mystical or imaginary world, beyond their own community. Books that are windows permit children to glimpse people, places and lives that are different from their own, potentially building empathy and understanding of difference. 'Mirrors' give the reader opportunity to see a reflection of their own lives and experiences, giving credence to lived experiences and realities. Mirror books allow children to see opportunities they could and should have. 'Sliding doors' provide the reader a doorway through which they can enter a completely different world or set of circumstances that have been created by the author of the book. Sliding door books create escapism, discovery and light up imagination (for further information on books as window, mirrors and sliding doors, see Cremin, Chapter 1).

For windows, mirrors and sliding doors in books to be accessible to children, there must be diversity. If children don't see themselves represented in the books they read at school then a barrier may be created, for the world of school and the world of books is not 'their' world. As Hurley (2005) puts it, a child may well ask the question, 'If I am not in the [book] at all what does that mean?' Increasing representation in books is one way to build a bridge between children's lived realities and school culture. Children come to school with existing constructs of how the world works, based on their experiences, culture and language (Wrigley, 2000). As teachers, our most effective pedagogies value these experiences of our learners and our books must represent the diversity of these experiences. Diversity is not just about race, but needs to include gender, culture, sexuality and societal differences. Considering the normative culture in England which focuses on white, middle-class perspectives, it is inevitable that the number of books with a main character who is, for example, a strong, confident female, transgender, from a Middle Eastern background or from a same-sex family will be less common.

Research focus

The Centre for Literacy in Primary Education (CLPE) (2019) have highlighted continued significant issues related to under-represented groups in children's literature. Of 11,011 children's books published in the UK in 2018, 743 featured BAME characters. Just 4 per cent of children's books published in 2018 had a BAME main character, and although this shows an increase from 1 per cent in 2017 there is clearly still significant progress to be made. Social justice issues were featured in 20 per cent of the books reviewed and, of these, 29 per cent focused on generic celebration of difference. While these kinds of books are important, it is essential that BAME representation is not solely confined to books that collate race with moral issues or debates and in which 'othering' narratives dominate.

The recent increases in BAME representation are to be welcomed, but should also be read with caution, as the report indicates that the quality of content and the characterisation of BAME representations in books remains concerning and, in some cases, alarming:

- over a quarter of the books reviewed only featured BAME as background characters;

- the representation of BAME characters compared to white characters was inequitable. For example, white characters were given more dialogue, BAME characters were portrayed inaccurately or marginalised, and BAME characters were more likely to be deployed as 'side-kicks' or for comedy value;

- pictorial representations of BAME characters also came under scrutiny. Some books contained BAME characters that had been drawn with exaggerated features that reduced them to caricatures. In other books, colourism was detected whereby a lighter skin tone of a character was positively correlated with their virtuousness;

- in both fictionalised and non-fiction historical books, portrayals of BAME figures were often over-simplified. Contentious parts of historical facts were glossed over or misrepresented, negating the realities of lived experiences for under-represented groups. This is an issue that speaks to the Black Lives Matter movement and calls to de-colonise the curriculum.

Case study: auditing books and improving representation

Sarah, a recently qualified teacher at a primary school in east Leeds, identified that the books in her 'inherited' classroom reading area were not representative of the community around the school and did not reflect the diversity of the children in her Year 1 class. She was aware that if the children could not see themselves represented in the stories they were reading, this

→

could impact upon their enjoyment of reading and, more long term, could affect their perceptions of their identity with consequences for their future life and employment prospects.

As a starting point, Sarah looked around the wider school and gathered a selection of high-quality, age-appropriate books, including well-known titles such as *Amazing Grace* by Mary Hoffman, *Handa's Surprise* by Eileen Browne, *Hue Boy* by Rita Phillips Mitchell and *Peter's Chair* by Ezra Jack Keats from the school library. The class, however, had children from a broad range of cultures and ethnicities, with 35 per cent of the children from a Middle Eastern background. Sarah realised that this was a real gap in school currently, finding very few books which would reflect these children. She contacted the local authority School Library Service, which she found would assemble crates of books for her school to borrow. She requested a topic box of culturally diverse books for five- to seven-year-olds to bridge the gap until she could start her own collection personalised for her class.

The children's voices were also an important factor. Having borrowed books initially, Sarah was able to monitor which books the children liked and felt most connected to. Recent additions to the book corner included *Under My Hijab* by Hena Khan, *Nadia's Hands* by Karen English and *Deep in the Sahara* by Kelly Cunnane. This strategy allowed her to focus her later 'shopping list' on books which would make a real difference to the children in her class. She commented on children becoming more excited about choosing books to look at, more motivated about reading – especially in taking books home to share with their families; she hopes that this will have an impact on self-confidence, feelings of belonging and aspiration in the longer term.

Book corners within a classroom should be places that children are drawn to and want to spend time in. Adults working in the classroom must know that they are providing a high-quality experience with outstanding provision. It is essential therefore that teachers undertake an audit of their own classroom reading area at regular intervals.

Activity

Explore your own book corner or reflect on a book corner/book box in a setting that you have experienced. Work through the questions below (Monoyiou and Symeondiou, 2016) and consider some of the comments from the CLPE report (2019). If necessary, you could discuss with colleagues in school or a liaison librarian how to make changes to what is on offer.

- Looking at the front cover, can children see that characters like themselves are going to be in the book?
- How are characters conceptualised as 'different' portrayed?
- What messages does the plot convey to the reader?

- Is the terminology up to date?
- Are there any messages (explicit or implicit) that reinforce minority oppression or stereotypes?
- How do illustrations complement the written text?
- Are there biographies and auto-biographies of positive diverse role models included?

Challenging stereotypes: what's 'normal'?

As seen in the case study above, increasing representation in response to a class context is important to build an inclusive culture. However, an issue to be aware of is the nature of many inclusive books, which feature subjects such as racism, disability or LGBTQ+ characters as 'issues' that need to be debated and explicitly addressed (Strick, 2013). These kinds of books can be helpful in supporting young people's awareness and helping them work through difficult situations. However, if the books that we use only ever problematise difference then we run the risk of (unintentionally) reproducing 'othering' narratives whereby stereotypes of 'us and them' dominate (Alemanji, 2017). Children shape their thinking and begin to understand multiple aspects of their identity through the books they read – what it means to be a boy or a girl, able-bodied or disabled, from an ethnic minority or dominant culture, and so on. In this context, 'realistic' representations are essential – that is, representations where characters are multidimensional and relatable rather than passive actors who are included for 'moralistic' lessons about tolerating difference.

An example of a book that promotes diversity through realistic representations is *Max the Champion* by Sean Stockdale and Alex Strick, a book about a little boy who loves sport. The images in the book contain people with a range of disabilities, but they are not presented as issues or problems to be resolved but interwoven into the story to normalise a full range of physical and mental capabilities. As Strick (2013) argues, a good, inclusive book shows disabled children (and adults) alongside their peers without defining them by their disability.

As teachers, we can begin to create safe spaces for children in under-represented groups by challenging deficit discourses and stereotypes, acknowledging our own limited knowledge and de-mystifying the realities of lived experiences (Goldstein, 2019). However, a significant concern for teachers can be perceived parental opposition to explicit teaching about diverse issues related to religion, gender and sexuality. For example, in recent years religious and conservative groups' protests outside primary schools to oppose a 'No Outsiders' diversity curriculum drew significant media attention (Parveen, 2019), along with legal challenges. However, when, as a teacher, you ask yourself: 'But what will the parents say?', check which parents you are thinking about. It could be useful to discuss this with colleagues so you can articulate your concerns. Are these parents who look like you? Are they white, straight and cisgender? Are they parents who have religious beliefs which contradict your own? Are you making assumptions about their reactions without checking in with them?

These considerations bring to the fore the importance of having honest conversations with parents and colleagues. A supportive, whole-school culture which promotes open conversations and involves senior leadership teams or experienced colleagues is ideal. Not everyone will be open-minded or will welcome conversations about diversity with primary-aged children. Teachers may need to frame content which could be considered challenging by some as focused on 'tolerance' and 'acceptance' in the early stages (Goldstein, 2019). One way to do this is by providing representation of diversity through children's books that are shared both in school and at home with parents and families. Using story books to introduce difficult or unfamiliar concepts can be a real support for initiating conversations about building a culture of acceptance where diversity is normalised.

Research focus

The No Outsiders project (No Outsiders, n.d.) in primary schools was piloted by Andrew Moffat in his own primary school in 2014 and was subsequently taken up by multiple primary schools across England. The No Outsiders curriculum includes a resource pack of 27 children's books, intended to explore themes related to gender and sexuality in an age-appropriate way. A significant focus of the project was to tackle dominant heteronormative (cisgender and straight) viewpoints in primary schools which could give rise to homophobic views. This means that the focus is not on school policies which punish homophobic language, and which can unwittingly reproduce 'othering' or deficit perspectives of homosexuality. Instead, the project seeks to build proactive approaches, including the use of LGBTQ+ literature, which has potential to promote empathy and understanding among pupils and to reorientate meanings of terms such as 'gay' and 'lesbian' to include recognisable and familiar people.

An example of a book commonly used in the project is *And Tango Makes Three* by Justin Richardson and Peter Parnell. This picture book recounts the famous story of two male penguins in New York's Central Park Zoo who adopt a penguin chick to raise together. The two penguin protagonists – Roy and Silo – are an accessible representation which may normalise alternatives to dominant cisgender/straight normative family expectations. Using this book – and other, similar examples from the No Outsiders resource list – is considered valuable in normalising same-sex relationships rather than problematising them (Mickenberg and Nel, 2011).

However, DePalma (2016) cautions us against assuming that any representation of minority groups is good representation. She takes issue with Roy and Silo as 'gay icons', pointing out that, taken alone, the book *And Tango Makes Three* may reinforce a binary of sexuality as straight or gay, and gender as male or female. As our understanding, and teaching, of gender and sexuality has developed, she argues, we need to consider less clearly defined gender

$\longrightarrow$

and sexual identities such as bisexual or transgender. However, this can be problematic, as Atkinson and Moffat (2009) report that teachers lack confidence in teaching about less tangible and less easily defined queer experiences. This means that a vast range of gender and sexuality identities may not be represented to primary-age children. Further, Epstein (2013), in analysis of 60 children's books, found that gay and lesbian characters were more likely to be represented than other forms of sexuality. The majority of gay and lesbian characters in the books she studied were also cisgender, white, middle class and able-bodied. As such, teachers should actively seek out books which include a range of gender and sexuality representations so as not to unwittingly reinforce hierarchies of gender and sexual identities which prioritise the norm as straight and cisgender.

Case study: using a book to explore gender identity

Aishah is Learning Mentor at a primary school in South Bradford. Her role gives her the opportunity to get to know the school community well and she is aware that diverse families are part of the school community. She supports children from families with two mums, two dads, re-constituted families and one family with a single, transgender parent.

She has an awareness that there may be children in school who are starting to struggle with gender identity. Aishah was keen to consider ways of ensuring that any such child would have the opportunity to feel comfortable with their feelings and be supported by seeing other children like themselves within the books they read. She also wanted cisgender children to be able to think beyond traditional gender stereotypes and become accepting of children who they may perceive as different or not quite the same as themselves.

Aishah approached the Year 3 class teacher to discuss her ideas and see whether he was interested in supporting her work with his class on a small-scale group project related to gender identity and exploring children's perceptions of gender. From conversations with colleagues, Aishah was aware that some teachers are quite reluctant to broach the topic of gender identity and felt there was the need for further training, resources and support for teachers to adequately facilitate the discussions about or the inclusion of transgender pupils. Many of her colleagues were uncertain about whether educating about gender identity in primary schools was 'age-appropriate' and commented on it being too early to have such discourses in terms of 'childhood innocence'.

Aishah believed that books could be a vehicle to start discussions with children in Key Stage 1. She chose to use a simple story book called *Sparkle Boy* by Lesléa Newman. The story has the main character, a boy called Casey, being a child who loves to do conventional 'boy' activities such as playing with construction blocks and a dumper truck, but also likes things that 'shimmer, glitter and sparkle'. The story explores individuality, acceptance and the idea that it is OK to just be yourself and who you feel happiest being. Aishah worked with the class teacher and they made the decision to use the comprehensive teacher guide and lesson plans

⟶

(Lee and Low, 2017) which go with the book to explore the text. The sessions went well, with children quickly moving from a position of discomfort at a boy wearing a shimmery skirt to acceptance of difference.

Both Aishah and the class teacher feel that they can start by increasing the range of books in class libraries to include those where gender binaries are challenged. They also intend to try to draw up their own teaching packs to go with other texts and they plan to deliver some CPD to school colleagues. They also plan to inform parents/carers and share books with families to build a community understanding and support.

Activity

Undertake some research online in relation to books for primary-aged children which challenge normative views of gender (binary) and sexuality (straight). There is an increasing number out there. You should be able to find at least one which you feel you could use with your class as part of a lesson.

One example is *King and King* by Linda de Haan and Stern Nijland, which is a different take on a traditional fairy story. The queen of a small, unnamed country encourages her son to choose a wife so that she can retire. The prince, who 'never cared much for princesses' caves in and agrees to get married. None of the potential brides appeal to him, until Princess Madeleine comes along. The prince falls in love, not with the princess, but with her brother, Prince Lee. A 'very special' wedding follows and, of course, everyone lives happily ever after.

Use the teachers' materials for *Sparkle Boy* by Lesléa Newman as a framework. What questions would you want to ask about your chosen book? What discussions would you instigate? What impact do you think this activity would have? How might you share this kind of book with parents and carers?

Learning outcomes review

Now that you have read this chapter, you should understand:

- some of the current issues related to diversity in terms of race, culture, gender, sexuality and [dis]ability;
- key factors to consider when choosing quality books which don't reproduce 'othering' narratives;
- the need to ensure all children are represented in the texts they read;
- the importance of choosing books which normalise difference rather than framing it as an issue or problem to be resolved.

Conclusion

Inclusive education is about challenging deficit discourses and promoting support for difference and diversity through normalising and representing minority groups. As teachers, we can help to build an inclusive culture by increasing representation in the books that we read and share with our children and their families. This means much more than a tokenistic approach where we might read a 'special' book for Black History Month or Pride week. It is our responsibility to carefully audit each book we choose to use with our children, ensuring authentic representation of a range of diverse, multidimensional characters. In selecting books, we need to be alert to the explicit and implicit messages that could be contained which reproduce inequalities. We also need to take care that we don't (unintentionally) reproduce stereotypes or promote binary norms which categorise people as male or female and straight or gay, rather than considering fluidity of various identities.

Of course, this all takes place in a school culture and context that promotes diversity and inclusion. Senior leaders need to support teachers in developing relationships with parents, carers and school communities, being mindful that some conversations about diversity in regards culture, race, religion, gender and sexuality could be difficult. But, as we have seen in this chapter, sharing a book could be a first doorway into initiating a difficult conversation, into helping a child see the future they could have, into creating a safe space for a child struggling with their identity. Books could and should be our most powerful tool for building diversity, inclusion and acceptance in our classrooms.

References

Alemanji, A.A. (2017) *Antiracism Education In and Out of Schools*. Palgrave Macmillan e-book. DOI: 10.1007/978-3-319-56315-2

Atkinson, E. and Moffat, A. (2009) Bodies and minds: essentialism, activism and strategic disruptions in the primary school and beyond, in R. DePalma and E. Atkinson (eds), *Interrogating Heteronormativity in Primary Schools: The No Outsiders Project*. London: Trentham. Available at: https://www.academia.edu/1029463/Interrogating_Heteronormativity_in_ Primary_Schools_The _No_Outsiders_Project (accessed 6 October 2020).

Bishop, R.S. (1990) Mirrors, windows and sliding glass doors. *Choosing and Using Books for the Classroom*, 6(3).

Centre for Literacy in Primary Education (CLPE) (2019) *Reflecting Realities: Survey of Ethnic Representation within UK Children's Literature 2018*. London: CLPE.

Chatfield, G. (2019) *How Gender Stereotypes in Children's Books Shape Career Choices* Available at: https://www.thersa.org/discover/publications-and-articles/rsa-blogs/2019/03/gender-books (accessed 15 June 2020).

Crenshaw, K. (1989) Demarginalizing the intersection of race and sex: a black feminist critique of antidiscrimination doctrine, feminist theory and anti-racist politics. University of Chicago Legal Forum, special issue: *Feminism in the Law: Theory, Practice and Criticism*, 139–68.

DePalma, R. (2016) Gay penguins, sissy ducklings … and beyond? Exploring gender and sexuality diversity through children's literature. *Discourse: Studies in the Cultural Politics of Education*, 37(6): 828–45.

DfE (2019) *National Statistics: Special Educational Needs in England: January 2019.* Available at: https://assets.publishing.service.gov.uk/government/uploads/system/uploads/attachment_data/file/814244/SEN_2019_Text.docx.pdf (accessed 15 June 2020).

Eaude, T. (2020) *Identity, Culture and Belonging: Educating Young Children for a Changing World.* Abingdon: Bloomsbury.

Education and Employers (2018) *Drawing the Future.* Available at: https://www.educationandemployers.org/drawing-the-future-published/ (accessed 15 June 2020).

Epstein, B.J. (2013) *Are the Kids All Right? Representations of LGBTQ Characters in Children's and Young Adult Literature.* Bristol: HammerOn Press.

Goldstein, T. (2019) *Teaching Gender and Sexuality at School: Letters to Teachers.* London and New York: Routledge.

Hurley, L.D. (2005) Seeing white: children of color and the Disney fairy tale princess. *The Journal of Negro Education*, 74(3): 221–32.

Kramer, M.A. (2001) Sex-role stereotyping in children's literature. Unpublished master's thesis, Pennsylvania State University, University Park, PA.

Lee and Low (2017) *Teacher's Guide: Sparkle Boy.* Lee and Low Books. Available at: https://www.leeandlow.com/uploads/loaded_document/433/Sparkle_Boy_TG.pdf (accessed 28 September 2020).

Mermelstein, A.D. (2018) Gender roles in children's literature and their influence on learners. *MinneTESOL Journal*, 34(2).

Mickenberg, J. and Nel, P. (2011) Radical children's literature now! *Children's Literature Association Quarterly*, 36: 445–73.

Monoyiou, E. and Symeonidou, S. (2016) The wonderful world of children's books? Negotiating diversity through children's literature. *International Journal of Inclusive Education*, 20(6): 588–603.

No Outsiders (n.d.) Available at: https://no-outsiders.com/ (accessed 28 September 2020).

Nuttall, A. and Doherty, J. (2014) Disaffected boys and the achievement gap: the 'wallpaper effect' and what is hidden by a focus on school results. *The Urban Review*, 46(5): 800–15.

Parveen, N. (2019) Parents complain to Manchester schools about LGBT lessons. *Guardian.* Available at: https://www.theguardian.com/education/2019/mar/19/fresh-complaints-about-lgbt-lessons-at-greater-manchester-primary-schools (accessed 28 September 2020).

Race, R. (ed.) (2017) *Advancing Multicultural Dialogues in Education.* Basingstoke: Palgrave Macmillan.

Reeves, A. and Kirk, P. (2018) *Why Gender Diversity in Children's Books Matters*. Available at: http://www.jkp.com/jkpblog/2018/03/gender-diverse-childrens-books/ (accessed 11 May 2020).

Runnymede Trust/NASUWT (2017) *Visible Minorities, Invisible Teachers: BME Teachers in the Education System in England*. Available at: https://www.nasuwt.org.uk/uploads/assets/uploaded/6576a736-87d3-4a21-837fd1a1ea4aa2c5.pdf (accessed 15 June 2020).

Singh, M. (1998) Gender Issues in Children's Literature. ERIC, Identifier: ED424591. Available at: http://www.indiana.edu/~reading/ieo/digests/d135.html (accessed 12 May 12 2020).

Strick, A. (2013) Is everybody in? A look at diversity and inclusion in children's books. *The School Librarian*, 61(3): 131–2.

Temple, C. (1993) What if 'Beauty' had been ugly? Reading against the grain of gender bias in children's books. *Language Arts*, 70(2): 89–93.

Wrigley, T. (2000) *The Power to Learn: Stories of Success in the Education of Asian and Other Bilingual Pupils*. Stoke-on-Trent: Trentham.

Further reading

Atthill, C. and Jha, J. (2009) *The Gender Responsive School: An Action Guide*. London: Commonwealth Secretariat.

Moffat, A. (2017) *No Outsiders in Our School: Teaching the Equality Act in Primary Schools*. Abingdon: Routledge.

8 Deeper Reading for EAL Pupils

Kulwinder Maude

Learning outcomes

By reading this chapter you will have considered:

- the key issues with learning to read in a second language;
- why it is important to understand top-down and bottom-up approaches to reading in a second language;
- how you can encourage deeper reading through dual language books and use of first language.

Teachers' Standards

5. Adapt teaching to respond to the strengths and needs of all pupils:

- know when and how to differentiate appropriately, using approaches which enable pupils to be taught effectively;
- have a secure understanding of how a range of factors can inhibit pupils' ability to learn, and how best to overcome these;
- have a clear understanding of the needs of all pupils, including ... those with English as an additional language; ... and be able to use and evaluate distinctive teaching approaches to engage and support them.

Curriculum links

Despite the ever-increasing number of multilingual pupils in both primary and secondary schools in England, the current National Curriculum does not specifically provide any guidance on how to teach EAL pupils. However, the National Curriculum Statutory Guidance (DfE, 2013), Section 4, sets out principles for the inclusion of all pupils, with two main requirements:

- setting suitable challenges;
- responding to pupils' needs and overcoming potential barriers for individuals and groups of pupils.

As part of the second requirement, two principles are stated (on p9) which relate specifically to EAL:

4.5 Teachers must also take account of the needs of pupils whose first language is not English. Monitoring of progress should take account of the pupil's age, length of time in this country, previous educational experience and ability in other languages.

4.6 The ability of pupils for whom English is an additional language to take part in the National Curriculum may be in advance of their communication skills in English. Teachers should plan teaching opportunities to help pupils develop their English and should aim to provide the support pupils need to take part in all subjects.

Defining terms

EAL stands for English as an additional language and recognises the fact that many children learning English in schools in this country already know one or more other languages and are adding English to that repertoire.

Bilingual is used to refer to those children who have access to more than one language at home and at school. It does not necessarily imply full fluency in both or all of their languages.

Introduction

More and more teachers find themselves teaching students from increasingly diverse linguistic and cultural backgrounds. According to recent figures (DfE, 2020), the proportion of EAL learners in schools rose to 21.3 per cent (primary) and 17.1 per cent (secondary). The biggest rise, however, is in the EYFS sector: 30.1 per cent. Given the multicultural and multilingual nature of our classrooms, it would be rare for a newly qualified teacher not to experience linguistic diversity in the classroom. Some of these experiences may be worrying to teachers with no knowledge of the children's language, no background or training in bilingual multicultural education, or no appropriate teaching materials. This chapter aims to contribute towards building understanding of second language acquisition. Two case studies will be used to highlight the role of classroom talk, first language and dual language books in developing a love for deeper reading in EAL pupils.

Before you attempt to understand reading in a second language, it will be beneficial to familiarise yourselves briefly with the research landscape. Historically, research in teaching and assessing reading in a second language can be seen as a continuum with psychological or cognitive approaches (McLaughlin, 1994) on one hand and reading as a social practice (Baker, 1996) on the other. The current National Curriculum in England promotes the cognitive approaches which focus on literacy, which is defined by Cline and Shamsi (2000, p13) as a psycholinguistic process involving methods such as, letter recognition, phonological encoding, decoding of grapheme strings, word recognition, etc. There is a further emphasis on the skills of reading and writing, which are divided into vocabulary, grammar and composition, etc. It is vital to say here that several researchers, including Vadasy and Sanders (2011) and Yeung *et al.* (2013) (in Jamaludin *et al.*, 2016), suggest cognitive approaches (blending and segmenting phonemes) may be effective in developing reading skills across languages. However, Yeung *et al.* (2013) (in Jamaludin *et al.*, 2016) also point out that applying their findings across different EAL contexts could be problematic and doubtful, due to the complexities of different language structures. Recent research (Foley *et al.*, 2018) into provision for EAL within teacher education has noted that the ways in which English, specifically literacy, is constructed in the National Curriculum is debatable and this has implications for EAL learners.

Let's unpick some of these implications in further detail. We know that EAL pupils move through the schooling years 'reading to learn' as well as 'learning to read'. For some, learning to decode the unfamiliar written script maybe problematic, for others, it maybe the unfamiliar content of the text that is a hindrance. Goodman (1967) proposed that a reader brings three types of knowledge to the text: *semantic* (knowledge of the world); *syntactic* (structure of language); and *graphophonic* (the letter–sound relationships). During early language development, young children bring in their already existing and ever-increasing knowledge of the world around them when making meaning. But it may not be the same for pupils who might not share the dominant culture or language and thereby, lack shared cultural or linguistic points of references for the target language (English in this instance). This has serious ramifications for pupils learning English as an additional language as they do not have access to a key reading tool of their monolingual counterparts: *previous knowledge*. Baker (1996) argued that in reading and writing we bring not only previous experiences, but also our values and beliefs, enabling us to create meaning from what we read and insert understanding into what we write. This socio-cultural approach to literacy may allow EAL pupils to create an appropriate cultural meaning when reading an unfamiliar text.

So what is the best way to teach reading in a second language?

Bottom-up versus top-down approaches

On the one hand, some approaches claim that a bottom-up approach, where children learn to make meaning with the most individual units of text (graphemes and phonemes), moving on to words and then whole texts, is the most successful way of teaching reading. Children often rely on repetition of whatever the 'sound symbols' of the texts are, along with a number of 'sight words', which are often carefully controlled. For EAL pupils, a major disadvantage with such phonics-driven approaches is that often there are few links or little previous knowledge about English or their own language that they can bring to the texts. The sounds of the key words may not match with the sounds of their first language. Gibbons (2009, p82) warned us that learning to read in a second language may become an abstract process, where unfamiliar knowledge (sounds of English) is used to teach an unfamiliar skill (reading in English). Along similar lines, although advocates of the 'simple view of reading' (see Stuart *et al.*, 2008) agree that comprehension skills need equal attention in the classroom, Paran and Wallace (2016) highlight that EAL pupils with limited comprehension skills may find themselves 'barking at print' (p23) if they can decode but not attach meaning to the text.

On the other hand, whole-word or top-down approaches encourage children to engage with meaning-making at the level of the whole text. The emphasis is on being able to recognise the type and purpose of text in order to predict meaning based on previous knowledge and experiences that a learner brings to the text. For EAL pupils, a major disadvantage of whole-word approaches is that they may not focus on language itself in sufficient depth. As mentioned above, Goodman (1967) sheds light on the role of three kinds of knowledge (semantic, syntactic and graphophonic) that a learner depends on in order to make predictions. EAL pupils may not have the culturally specific knowledge or know enough about the structure of the language or meaning of words which signpost transition, for example, *although, however, consequently*. This may help in explaining why dependence on just whole-word approaches may result in a breakdown of the reading process for some EAL pupils.

Research focus

There has been some consensus about the best way to teach reading. Researchers now argue that both bottom-up and top-down skills can be useful in developing successful EAL readers. However, Wallace (2014, p8) argues that over the years, the need for developing a language-rich repertoire has been sacrificed for focus on how language is pronounced (evident in the phonics-driven approaches). For teachers of EAL pupils, it is important to develop understanding of how to support children in accessing meaning in a text.

Regardless of whether your school follows the bottom-up or top-down (whole-word) approach or a mixture of both approaches to facilitate reading in a second language, EAL pupils need access to a multitude of opportunities to read and engage in 'talk' within the classroom. Freebody and Luke (1990) emphasised development of four components of literacy success and argue that successful readers should be able to take on the roles of: *code breaker* (decoding); *text participant* (bring in previous knowledge); *text user* (participate in discussion

→

around the written text); and *text analyst* (understand the implicit meaning of the text). Given that EAL is not recognised as a distinct discipline within the curriculum in the UK, the fact that EAL pupils are not only learning a new language, but also new content *in* and *through* the new language, is often forgotten.

Activity

Gibbons (2015) in her book *Scaffolding Language Scaffolding Learning*, chapter 6, introduces in great detail various practical strategies that can be used in the classroom to encourage EAL pupils to engage with reading at a deeper level. It would be extremely beneficial to engage with her writing in depth and try some of the strategies in your classroom teaching. In the meantime, here are a few strategies that you might like to try:

- before reading activities – prediction from a picture or visuals or key words; personal narratives; semantic web; reader questions; sequencing illustrations; skeleton text (outline of a text is there but key information is missing) and previewing the text (provide explicit information about the content beforehand);
- during reading – scanning for information; pause and predict; margin questions; scaffolding a detailed reading; reading critically; language analysis; questioning the text;
- after reading strategies – true/false statements; graphic outlines; summarising the text; cloze activities; sentence reconstruction; jumbled words; innovating on the text.

Case study: developing reading comprehension with Year 2 EAL children

The school in this case study serves a multicultural community, with the proportion of pupils coming from minority ethnic backgrounds being far higher than average. It is a very large primary school with an intake of more than 800 pupils. Less than a third are white British, with the largest ethnic groups being Somali, black African and Asian Indian. The school was served a 'notice to improve' in 2016 following an inspection. Reading attainment of EAL pupils in particular was one of the causes for concern. Here is an example of how the specialised EAL teacher focused on developing reading comprehension with Year 2 EAL children. The pupils identified for intervention were generally of mixed proficiency in English. Some could demonstrate and understand basic punctuation; could read simple sentences; refer to visual clues in texts; re-tell main points from a text which placed them at 'working towards the expected level' at KS1 according to the National Curriculum. Some pupils could be placed at the expected level for KS1 reading as they could describe the setting of a story; could select relevant text to answer questions or sometimes respond to how/why questions related to a text but not consistently.

→

The following exemplar system of work was developed to be used with any commercial book programme. Seven lessons were planned which could be taught once a week, or every day, depending on the school timetable arrangements. This system can be a useful resource for newly qualified teachers, who often express anxiety about not knowing how to develop early reading outside regular phonics instruction.

Learning focus	Activities	Resources
• To be able to produce some recognisable letters • To be able to read some high-frequency words and familiar words fluently and automatically • To be able to decode familiar and some unfamiliar words using blending as the prime approach • To be aware of punctuation marks – e.g. pausing at full stops	• Practise handwriting (allocated time 5–10 mins). Model how to hold a pencil effectively • Teach how to control size, shape and orientation in writing English alphabets • CVC words flash cards – show cards, model saying the words clearly with the correct accent. Ask the children to repeat after the teacher. Play bingo/snap linked with the key words in the reading book or the target CVC words • Match word to object by reading • Read the words around the class • Sounding out the words using a '/' to denote that they have sounded it out • Model reading the selected text taking account of the punctuation, meaning and speech. Develop some sign to indicate full stops and praise the children every time they demonstrate that they have noticed one	• Copies of the selected text • Record sheets • Flash cards for CVC words • Plastic wallets and folders
Learning focus	Activities	Resources
• To be able to copy over/under a model • To be able to read some words fluently • To be able to recall some simple points from the text read • To be able to locate some pages/sections of interest, e.g. favourite characters, events, info, pictures	• Practise handwriting and CVC words as above • Read selected texts – sequence sentences and pictures from familiar texts • Retelling a story in a reading group • Simple 'wh' questions • Role play • Find page about the x • Ask children to find information about xyz if reading a non-fiction text • Write a simple book review • Draw your favourite character/part of the book • Write a fact about the subject in the book – non-fiction book • Write the page number next to the picture – non-fiction text	• Same as above

→

Learning focus	Activities	Resources
• To be able to imitate adults' writing and understand the purpose of writing • To be able to derive reasonable inference at a basic level • To be able to comment about the meaning of parts of the text, e.g. details of illustrations/ diagrams, changes in font	• Practise handwriting and CVC words as above • Look at the picture and imagine what the character is saying/thinking – the teacher can scribe if the child can't write • Look at the speech and ask 'Who says …?' • Ask questions like 'Why is the picture there?'; 'Why is that in bold?' • Use the picture to find out what they can understand about the text – e.g. 'What can you tell me about the car?' • Ask the children to fill in the speech bubbles • Ask the children to fill in faces to show emotion • Colour code a page for features – e.g. title in red, diagram in blue, etc.	• Same as above

Learning focus	Activities	Resources
• To be able to form letters/ words correctly independently • To develop some awareness of meaning of simple text features – font style, labels, titles	• Practise handwriting and CVC words as above • ICT focus – create titles, captions and labels for a text focusing on font • Ask questions like: 'What is this called?', pointing to various parts of a book or text • Put in missing captions, labels and titles, etc.	• Same as above

Learning focus	Activities	Resources
• To be able to ascribe meaning to own marking ('read what has been written') • To be able to comment on obvious features of language – rhymes, refrains, significant words and phrases	• Practise handwriting and CVC words as above • Encourage the children to identify any repeating parts • Ask them to explain what it means • Stress on finding words which tell us the most about the character/feelings/what will happen next • Ask children 'Why does he say "xyz"?'	• Same as above

Learning focus	Activities	Resources
• To be able to write simple regular words	• Practise handwriting and CVC words as above • In each text ask children to explain their favourite part. Sort books previously read into piles of like/dislike	• Same as above

Learning focus	Activities	Resources
• To be able to comment about preferences … mostly linked to own experiences	• Encourage children to speak in full sentences about what they like or dislike in the text • Introduce competition by encouraging children to choose as many sentences or words used to describe as they can in under a minute	• Same as above
Learning focus	Activities	Resources
• To be able to have a phonic attempt at words and write independently • To be able to identify and distinguish basic features of a well-known story and information texts – 'What typically happens to good or bad characters?' etc.	• Practise handwriting and CVC words as above • Predict based on experience – e.g. in a series of reading books • Predict what the writing will be about on an information text page • Predict how a story will start – e.g. a traditional role • Cover up parts of an information text and guess what is underneath	• Same as above

Activity

- You will notice that the above scheme of work focused not just on reading, but also some writing in a small group setting. Think about the interconnectivity of speaking, listening, reading and writing here. We know that mastery of one is not a prerequisite for encouraging development of the other three aspects.
- How can the above scheme of work be used with newly arrived EAL pupils in KS2? Focus on how you can incorporate strategies suggested in Gibbons (2015, chapter 6) into your everyday teaching of reading.
- The EAL teacher encouraged a lot of *talk* within the group. How did that help with developing reading comprehension in a second language?

The role of talk in second language acquisition

Vygotsky (1978) viewed interactive language as a communication tool which had the potential to empower learners. Similarly, Gibbons (1998) viewed the classroom as a place where *joint* construction of meaning took place through the medium of *joint* understandings and *joint* language reached between the teacher and the pupils. Swain (1995) concurred in favour of the importance of providing opportunities to EAL pupils to modify, reformulate and practise new language with an aim to produce more coherent and syntactically improved discourse. More recently, Mercer and Howe (2012) noticed that when teachers engaged in effective questioning where they encouraged pupils to explain and elaborate their thinking, this helped in developing reading comprehension. From a second language perspective, classroom talk provides such a platform where EAL pupils can answer questions and engage in conversations around a particular text. Ludhra and Jones (2008, p59) remind us that it is often during classroom talk and discussions that EAL pupils' implicit thoughts and ideas 'click' into place. Thus, it can be argued that the quality of classroom discourse is a powerful indicator of reading development in an additional language.

Next, let us consider the role of dual language books in facilitating deeper reading through the medium of classroom talk. Western education systems often assume that pre-school children acquire language when they are read to by their parents and that the spoken language is well developed mostly by the time children start school. This already acquired knowledge is built on further through systematic instruction in school. However, this may not be the case with EAL pupils. This is where pictorial dual language books based on commonly known stories can be extremely beneficial in facilitating that early language development. Dual language books (DLB), for example, *The Very Hungry Caterpillar; Gruffalo; Brown Bear, Brown Bear; What Do You See?; Aliens Love Underpants*; and *Handa's Surprise* (all available via Mantralingua) are published in various different languages (Arabic, Punjabi, Farsi, Somali, German, French, Chinese, Urdu, etc.). DLBs can not only facilitate story reading by providing visual cues along with the written text, but also encourage parental involvement in the children's education. Ma (2008) highlighted that parents of EAL pupils need to be a part of the English-speaking world of their children while children also develop proficiency in their first language. This reminds us of Vygotsky's socio-cultural theory where EAL pupils need to interact with both cultures in order to develop proficiency in both languages.

Case study: dual language books for bilingual pupils

Story book reading is one of the most widely recommended ways to help young children learn about literacy. The more access children have to books at a young age, the better. However, access to appropriate books can be an issue, especially when the home language and culture are different from the dominant language in school. One school in the south east of England addressed this issue by engaging with dual language books for their bilingual pupils in Year 3 and Year 4. Based on the majority language groups and adult support available within the year groups, dual language books in Polish, Punjabi, Urdu and Arabic were used for seven weeks during the guided reading sessions. The teachers recruited parent volunteers, who were given training in the suggested nature of questions and foci for the dual language books. Burgoyne *et al.* (2013) reiterate that while limited vocabulary can hinder developing deeper reading, lack of appropriate background knowledge also holds EAL pupils back. Keeping this in mind, the dual language books selected were chosen on the basis of familiarity with the stories.

$\longrightarrow$

As indicated in published research (Sneddon, 2009; Naqvi *et al.*, 2013), the children gained substantially from the development of metalinguistic awareness and their graphophonic knowledge of the English language. Although children were reluctant to use their first language in the classroom discussions initially, they soon felt comfortable and successful in solving comprehension-related problems within the stories. Most children started bringing in their knowledge of other stories within their cultural repertoire and made comparisons between the English vocabulary and their first languages. The teachers noticed additional information from different cultural backgrounds appearing in the related writing tasks, which added depth and originality to their writing. Although teachers could not possibly learn all the languages of the classroom, they could connect with the children and parents through DLBs, thus strengthening identities while promoting *biliteracy* (Naqvi *et al.*, 2013, p7). In fact, Conteh (2018) points out that recent research focusing on *translanguaging* (oral interactions in multiple languages) ties in well with Hall and Cook's (2012) research on *own-language use*. Further engagement with such research may be beneficial for new teachers. (See further reading list for more details at the end of the chapter.)

Activity

- Nowadays dual language books are not just literal translation of the text, but writers take into account the cultural nuances and traditions of both languages. Familiarise yourself with the Mantralingua website, https://uk.mantralingua.com/dual-language-books-whistle-stop-tour, and experiment with some texts in your classroom.
- Explore how dual language books can be useful in helping KS2 pupils to make comparisons with the use of picture books in developing deeper reading.
- Are there any limitations to using dual language books in the classroom? Read some relevant articles mentioned at the end of the chapter to develop your understanding further.

Research focus

Ma (2008) highlighted that dual language books provided a platform to use first language within the classroom as a 'cultural tool' to facilitate the meaning-making process. The discussion, facilitated through dual language books, aims to provide the same benefits to EAL pupils as the shared language and cultural repertoire that monolingual English-speaking children bring into the classroom. As a result, EAL pupils may become more sensitive to deeper reading within context and become aware of how language can be manipulated to express themselves. Cummins (1986) identified factors like acknowledging first language and culture

$\longrightarrow$

in the school life as key in developing later academic language proficiency. From research on Spanish- and English-speaking bilingual pupils, Madrinan (2014) concluded that the use of first language helped EAL pupils make connections with their existing knowledge of the mother tongue, which in turn facilitated the process of understanding. Therefore, the teacher's role in planning in order to incorporate first language and culture into their teaching is crucial in developing language proficiency.

Learning outcomes review:

Now that you have read this chapter you should understand:

- the key issues with learning to read in a second language;
- why it is important to understand top-down and bottom-up approaches to reading in a second language;
- how you can encourage deeper reading through dual language books and use of first language.

Conclusion

Rigg and Allen (1989) rightly said that second language, just like first language, develops globally not linearly. So it is vital that EAL pupils are given opportunities to engage with language through meaningful contexts where they can refine their initial thoughts through classroom talk. In this chapter, you were introduced to some concepts of second-language acquisition. The first case study focused on how teachers could support EAL pupils with limited reading proficiency, or those working towards National Curriculum expectations KS1 or KS2. An alternative to reading schemes available commonly in the market is presented. It is suggested that picture books with vivid illustrations and stories with predictable patterns and repetitive language can help deepen reading comprehension for EAL pupils. Dual language books can serve as a vehicle for development of metalinguistic and socio-cultural awareness linked with language development in both languages. Finally, as Conteh (2018) asserts, teachers in England should be encouraged to develop understanding of *translanguaging* in order to facilitate second-language acquisition and deeper reading for EAL pupils.

References

Baker, C. (1996) *Foundations of Bilingual Education and Bilingualism* (2nd edn). Clevedon: Multilingual Matters.

Burgoyne, K., Whiteley, H. and Hutchinson, J. (2013) The role of background knowledge in text comprehension for children learning English as an additional language. *Journal of Research in Reading*, 36(2): 132–48.

Cline, T. and Shamsi, T. (2000) *Language needs or special needs? The assessment of learning difficulties in literacy among children learning English as an additional language: a literature review*. Research report no. 184. Department for Education and Employment.

Conteh, J. (2018) Translanguaging. *ELT Journal*, 72(4): 445–7.

Cummins, J. (1986) Empowering minority students: a framework for intervention. *Harvard Educational Review*, 56: 18–36.

Department for Education (DfE) (2011) *Teachers' Standards in England*. London: DfE. Available at: https://assets.publishing.service.gov.uk/government/uploads/system/uploads/attachment_data/file/665520/Teachers__Standards.pdf (accessed 8 July 2020).

Department for Education (2013) *The National Curriculum in England: Key Stages 1 and 2 Framework Document*. Available at: https://www.gov.uk/government/publications/national-curriculum-in-england-primary-curriculum (accessed 30 April 2020).

Department for Education (2014) *National Curriculum in England: Framework for Key Stages 1 to 4*. London: DfE. Available at: https://www.gov.uk/government/publications/national-curriculum-in-england-framework-for-key-stages-1-to-4 (accessed 8 July 2020).

Department for Education (2020) *Schools, Pupils and their Characteristics*. Available at: https://explore-education-statistics.service.gov.uk/find-statistics/school-pupils-and-their-characteristics (accessed 8 July 2020).

Foley, Y., Anderson, C., Conteh, J. and Hancock, J. (2018) *English as an Additional Language and Initial Teacher Education*. University of Edinburgh. Available at: http://www.ceres.education.ed.ac.uk/wp-content/uploads/ITE-Report.pdf (accessed 8 July 2020).

Freebody, P. and Luke, A. (1990) 'Literacies' programs: Debates and demands in cultural context. *Prospect*, 5: 7–16.

Gibbons, P. (1998) Classroom talk and the learning of new registers in a second language. *Language and Education*, 12(2): 99–118. DOI: 10.1080/09500789808666742.

Gibbons, P. (2009) *English Learners, Academic Literacy, and Thinking*. Portsmouth, NH: Heinemann.

Gibbons, P. (2015) *Scaffolding Language Scaffolding Learning: Teaching English Language Learners in the Mainstream Classroom* (2nd edn). Portsmouth, NH: Heinemann.

Goodman, K. (1967) Reading: a psycholinguistic guessing game. *Journal of the Reading Specialist*, 6(4): 126–35.

Hall, G. and Cook, G. (2012) Own-language use in language teaching and learning. *Language Teaching*, 45(3): 271–308.

Jamaludin, K., Alias, N., Khir, R., DeWitt, D. and Kenayathulka, B. (2016) The effectiveness of synthetic phonics in the development of early reading skills amongst struggling young ESL readers. *School Effectiveness and School Improvement*, 27(3): 455–70.

Ludhra, G. and Jones, D. (2008) Conveying the 'right' kind of message: planning for the first language and culture within the primary classroom. *English Teaching: Practice and Critique*, 7.

Ma, J. (2008) 'Reading the word and the world': how mind and culture are mediated through the use of dual-language storybooks. *Education*, 36: 237–51.

Madrinan, M. (2014) The use of first language in the second-language classroom: a support for second language acquisition. *Gist Education and Learning Research Journal*. ISSN 1692-5777 (9) (July–December): 50–66.

McLaughlin, B. (1994) First and second language literacy in the late elementary grades, in B. McLeod (ed.), *Language and Learning: Educating Linguistically Diverse Students*. Albany: State University of New York Press, pp179–98.

Mercer, N. and Howe, C. (2012) Explaining the dialogic processes of teaching and learning: the value and potential of sociocultural theory. *Learning, Culture and Social Interaction*, 1(1): 12–21.

Naqvi, R., McKeogh, A., Thorne, K.J. and Pfitscher, C. (2013) Dual-language books as an emergent-literacy resource: culturally and linguistically responsive teaching and learning. *Journal of Early Childhood Literacy*, 13(4): 501–28.

Paran, A. and Wallace, C. (2016) Teaching literacy, in G. Hall (ed.), *The Routledge Handbook of English Language Teaching*. London: Routledge.

Rigg, P. and Allen, V. (eds) (1989) *When They Don't All Speak English: Integrating the ESL Student into the Regular Classroom*. Champaign, IL: NCTE.

Sneddon, R. (2009) *Bilingual Books – Biliterate Children: Learning to Read through Dual Language Books*. Stoke on Trent: Trentham.

Stuart, M., Stainthorp, R. and Snowling, M. (2008) Literacy as a complex activity: deconstructing the simple view of reading. *Literacy*, 42: 59–66.

Swain, M. (1995) Three functions of output in second language learning, in G. Cook and B. Seidlhofer (eds), *Principle and Practice in Applied Linguistics*. Oxford: Oxford University Press, 125–44.

Vadasy, P.F., and Sanders, E.A. (2011) Efficacy of supplemental phonics-based instruction for low-skilled first graders: how language minority status and pretest characteristics moderate treatment response. *Scientific Studies of Reading*, 15: 471–97.

Vygotsky, L.S. (1978) *Mind and Society*. Cambridge, MA: Harvard University Press.

Wallace, C. (2014) EAL Pupils in London Schools: A Success Story Against the Odds – Inaugural Professorial Lectures. London: Institute of Education Press.

Yeung, S.S.S., Siegel, L.S. and Chan, C.K.K. (2013) Effects of a phonological awareness program on English reading and spelling among Hong Kong Chinese ESL children. *Reading and Writing*, 26: 681–704.

Further reading

Anglia Ruskin University, University of Cambridge and the Bell Foundation (2014) School Approaches to the Education of EAL Students: Language Development, Social Integration and Achievement. Available at: https://www.educ.cam.ac.uk/research/projects/ealead/Fullreport.pdf (accessed 21 August 2020).

Centre for Literacy in Primary Education (CLPE) (2019) *Reflecting Realities: Survey of Ethnic Representation within UK Children's Literature 2018*. London: CLPE.

Conteh, J. (2019) *The EAL Teaching Book: Promoting Success for Multilingual Learners* (Primary Teaching Now). London: SAGE.

Crosse, K. (2007) *Introducing English as an Additional Language to Young Children*. London: SAGE.

Flynn, N. (2017) Language and literacy for children who are English language learners (ELLs): developing linguistically responsive teachers, in Goodwin, P. (ed.), *The Literate Classroom* (4th edn). Abingdon: Routledge, pp87–100.

Horst, M. (2005) Learning L2 vocabulary through extensive reading: a measurement study. *The Canadian Modern Language Review*, 61(3): 355–82. Available at: https://doi.org/10.1353/cml.2005.0018 (accessed 21 August 2020).

Jubileebooks.co.uk (2000–20) Available at: http://www.jubileebooks.co.uk/page/dual_language (accessed 9 July 2020).

Krashen, S. and Bland, J. (2014) Compelling comprehensible input, academic language and school libraries. *CLELEjournal*, 2(2).

Mantralingua.com (2002) Available at: https://uk.mantralingua.com/ (accessed 9 July 2020).

University of Oxford, with the Bell Foundation and Unbound Philanthropy (2018) *English as an Additional Language, Proficiency in English and Pupils' Educational Achievement: An Analysis of Local Authority Data*. Available at: https://www.bell-foundation.org.uk/research-report/english-as-an-additional-language-proficiency-in-english-and-pupils-educational-achievement-an-analysis-of-local-authority-data/ (accessed 21 August 2020).

9 The Diverse Reading Environment, including Visual and Graphic Literacies

Angela Gill, Stefan Kucharczyk and Catherine Lenahan

Learning outcomes

By reading this chapter you will have considered:

- debates around becoming literate in the 21st century;
- some of the rewards of teaching film in primary literacy;
- strategies for teaching children to read a film;
- how the meaningful development of the wider reading environment is influential in supporting readers of all ages and stages;
- why the adult role is essential to reading for meaning within any reading environment.

Teachers' Standards

2. Promote good progress and outcomes by pupils:

- demonstrate knowledge and understanding of how pupils learn and how this impacts on teaching.

3. Demonstrate good subject and curriculum knowledge:

- have a secure knowledge of the relevant subject(s) and curriculum areas, foster and maintain pupils' interest in the subject, and address misunderstandings
- demonstrate a critical understanding of developments in the subject and curriculum areas, and promote the value of scholarship
- demonstrate an understanding of and take responsibility for promoting high standards of literacy, articulacy and the correct use of standard English, whatever the teacher's specialist subject

4. Plan and teach well-structured lessons:

- promote a love of learning and children's intellectual curiosity.

5. Adapt teaching to respond to the strengths and needs of all pupils:

- know when and how to differentiate appropriately, using approaches which enable pupils to be taught effectively.

Curriculum links

All pupils must be encouraged to read widely across both fiction and non-fiction to develop their knowledge of themselves and the world in which they live, to establish an appreciation and love of reading, and to gain knowledge across the curriculum.

Reading widely and often increases pupils' vocabulary because they encounter words they would rarely hear or use in everyday speech.

Pupils should be taught to read fluently, understand extended prose (both fiction and non-fiction) and be encouraged to read for pleasure.

Introduction

In this chapter, we will explore how children engage in activities that promote reading for meaning and pleasure in the wider environment and how teachers might enable children to do so. As we have discovered in Chapter 6 of this book, poetry and drama can be effective tools in developing a love of language. In Chapter 4, we found out how the creative curriculum can promote and develop a love of books. In this chapter, we will focus on two keys things that can have a significant influence on the lives of children: film and the reading environment. In this multimodal era, we will explore how these two elements can develop children's literacy skills and their levels of engagement, influence reading for meaning and contribute to the development of a love of books.

Reading film and 21st-century literacy

This section of the chapter will explore how teaching primary learners to be *cine-* or *vide-literate* (to read moving visual images) challenges outdated definitions of literacy, celebrates and promotes the pleasure of stories and offers a means to better prepare children for living in the 21st century.

As well as its well-documented capacity to support learning, film is enjoyed by many as a source of storytelling entertainment. Cultural prejudices remain, however, and film (and other visual forms of literature) is often deemed inferior and having less cultural and educational worth than the printed word. But this comparison is not a comfortable one. Watching a film and reading a book are different experiences that require and draw upon different skills. Yet, as will be shown, being taught to 'read' film, and value the experience, can promote a broader appreciation of what it means to be a reader.

Reading the visual: a skill for the 21st century

It has been argued that the ability to read non-print forms of literature – that is, visual media such as film, television and computer games – is an essential skill for living, learning and thriving in the 21st century (UNESCO, 2015; BFI, 2008). This reflects both the ubiquity of moving, digital images in our daily lives and the potential of such skills for building capacity for cultural enrichment, critical enquiry and self-expression.

Although much has been written about the declining hours children spend reading (National Literacy Trust, 2020), children's screen-time habits are as popular as ever (Davis, 2019). This should not be a surprise. Technology has always shaped the way humans communicate, and film, in particular, has been transformed by advances in digital technology. No longer do we need to go into a darkened auditorium to watch a film: we have screens in every room of our houses, on our streets and in our classrooms. Today's young people have not needed to adapt to these changes: they were born into a 'bain d'image', *a bath of images* (Avgerinou, 2009). The prevalence of film and moving-image media in both society and children's cultural lives should challenge educators to rethink both what it means to read and what it means to be literate.

Rethinking 'literacy'

While technology has advanced, education has been slow to adapt. Although fluency in reading the printed word is rightly celebrated and encouraged, the National Curriculum for England (DfE, 2013) makes no mention of film, or other forms of digital media in relation to reading and literacy. This absence is a missed opportunity. Children may be left with an incomplete view of what it means to 'read' and feel unequipped, or not permitted, to interrogate or critique things they watch (NCTE, 2019). As film and television are a significant aspect of children's personal, cultural experiences, and have a key role in how they learn outside of school, the absence of film from school curricula seemingly invalidates this experience (Parry, 2013) and demeans something they find pleasurable. Ultimately, we must ask if a person can be truly literate in the 21st century without these skills, a question that has powerful implications for practitioners in Early Years and primary education where the foundations of literacy are laid.

While film finds some use in classrooms, such as being a motivational hook to a writing topic, it has been argued that some practitioners still judge watching a film as an activity intellectually less challenging and culturally less worthy than reading a print text (Parker, 1999; Parry and Bulman, 2017). This is despite the fact that the case for embedding film as a core aspect of literacy teaching has been well made: it can influence how children play (Smidt, 2010) and how they understand narrative both in reading and writing (Parry, 2013; Kucharczyk, 2016).

Learning to appreciate film has a greater reach than the classroom. Being taught to understand an author's craft can foster a deeper love for reading books, and so too learning to read film can promote cinema as an enjoyable and, culturally, a meaningful and enriching act. This is a shift that could have far-reaching implications for learners, especially those who find reading challenging or those who have distanced themselves from reading books for pleasure. Learning to read film *for pleasure* and to see value in this experience, as many adults do, perhaps offers a route towards confidence in engaging with literature and narrative. Even so, traditional views of the priorities of literacy teaching have endured and film is yet to find its place in education.

Activity: teaching aspects of film

The prevalence of film as a core aspect of literacy teaching depends as much on cultural and professional attitudes as it does practicalities: these might include the skills to teach film as a craft, the accessibility and availability of suitable films to show and the technology to show them. This, then, is an appropriate moment to critically reflect on what part film has to play in how literacy is taught in your setting. You might start by watching one of the recommended films suggested on p138 and p139 and try to see it both as a form of entertainment and a means of broadening understandings of reading and literacy.

Consider:

- how confident would you be in teaching aspects of a film to children?
- what might be the challenges and rewards in doing so?
- what obstacles might there be in establishing this kind of learning as part of your teaching practice?
- to what extent does your definition of literacy privilege the printed word? How willing would you be to alter this?

Research focus: multiliteracies

Society changes, but our essential need to communicate and to understand does not. As technological developments create new forms of media, the skills we need to make meaning from

→

them – our *literacies* – necessarily change (NCTE, 2019). As a reassessment of existing definitions of literacy that privilege the printed word, the concept of 'multiliteracies' considers the
many ways that information is analysed, shared and communicated (New London Group, 1996;
Cope and Kalantzis, 2015).

Some of these new literacies are directly related to how we watch and enjoy films. *Visual
literacy* can be described as a broad set of skills that enables learners to evaluate and
construct meaning from visual books – commonly multimodal picture books and graphica – for
the purposes of creative expression and aesthetic enjoyment (Avgerinou and Ericson, 1997;
Lundy and Stephens, 2015; Pantaleo, 2015).

The concept of *digital literacy* builds on this idea, but through the lens of digital technology
such as film, television and computer games. Discussions around *digital literacy*, Buckingham
(2015) argues, are too often concerned with technical competency or computer skills rather
than the emotional and interpretive uses of digital media. If children are to develop a critical
understanding, digital media need to be considered as something more than just a source
of information. Indeed, the British Film Institute (BFI) has advocated *cineliteracy* through the
systematic teaching of the skills and knowledge to enable both the appreciation and creation
of moving-image films in secondary schools (BFI, 2000).

While these terms might seem like a collection of niche buzzwords disconnected from
educational practice, they do represent a growing body of opinion that current definitions of
literacy are anachronistic and out of step with children's personal and cultural experiences.
Perhaps none of these terms adequately conveys the process of reading meaning into an ever
more diverse range of moving-image media. Instead, we might think of *vide-literacy* – the
ability to analyse and respond to different forms of complex digital, visual narratives which
may include film, but also augmented reality, virtual reality, gaming and internet-based
videos.

Reading a film

Watching a film is an absorbing and multisensory aesthetic experience with a rich heritage.
In a way that an author might describe a character's inner turmoil or the terrain of an alien
planet, a film can allow you to see and hear it as imagined by an artist: the filmmaker. A film
can be 'read' for the story being told, but also 'read' for *how* it is told. Both of these readings
are equally important.

While children are certainly familiar with the form of film, it should not be assumed that
exposure alone has made them aware of the finer aspects of a filmmaker's craft. Learning
to read the subtle meta-language of film – lighting, sound, *mise en scène* (see below) and

so on – can enable children to appreciate film as an independent art form, deepen their understanding of narrative and, importantly, broaden their ability to 'read' both printed books and the world around them.

While we hope that this chapter has argued convincingly for the relevance of introducing film into literacy teaching, teachers might feel daunted by the prospect. With this in mind, the next section offers an introduction to some of the key areas of film production and analysis. This is by no means a comprehensive guide and suggested further reading can be found in Chapter 10. This, however, should act as a taster for how analysing films can be taught to children.

A note about terminology: in this section 'shot' means a piece of recorded film; 'frame' means the arrangement of a film shot.

Figure 9.1   An image from 5 mètres 80 (High Diving Giraffes) Nicolas Deveaux, Cube Productions (2012)

Mise en scène

In filmmaking, some of the main elements are collectively known as *mise en scène*, which translates as *putting on the stage*. Some of the main aspects of *mise en scène* are described below.

Lighting and colour

Filmmakers use lighting to suggest the tone or mood of a scene in a film to the viewer. A setting that is lit in muted or dark colours can suggest oppression, unhappiness or foreboding; it might identify a villainous character, or a genre like horror. If warm, bright lighting is used, then this might show a character is loving or heroic, a place is safe or optimistic, or that we are watching a comedy or an adventure story.

You might ask the children to consider the predominant colour in a scene and what the filmmaker is trying to tell us by it; how lighting or colour can indicate genre; how colour changes for different characters or different parts of the story.

Suggested films: The Clock Tower, USA, 2008; *Sometimes the Stars*, Australia, 2010.

Placement, expression and movement

The placement of people or objects in a camera shot is one of the key aspects of *mise en scène*. Partly this is to do with how we read an actor's facial expressions and body language, but it can also relate to how characters and objects are framed by the screen. It is always chosen intentionally by the filmmaker. For example, a main character might be shown closer to the camera or in the centre of a shot; lonely characters might be shown from afar against an empty landscape; dynamic characters moving against a still backdrop.

Here, you might ask children to consider where the characters are in the frame and what this tells us about them; how different characters move; how the placement and movement of the main hero compares or contrast to that of the main villain.

Suggested films: Jotun: Journey of a Viking, France, n.d.; *Ruin*, USA, 2011.

Cinematography

Cinematography is concerned with how the arranged shot, the *mise en scène*, is captured on film. Again, these are deliberate choices both to convey the plot and to indicate to viewers how they should feel about a place, character or their actions.

Camera techniques

The camera is much more than a piece of technical equipment: it is the lens through which the filmmaker shows us the action taking place. Just as an author chooses to draw our attention to certain details of a story – the character's appearance, for example – a filmmaker does this through the choice of camera shot. Even in animated films such as *Spirited Away* or *Finding Nemo*, there is still a sense of a camera following the action even though it is not physically there. Some of the main camera techniques used are as follows:

Close-up   A character's face fills the screen. Used to create intensity, show emotional reaction and identify a main character.

Long shot	An actor is filmed from a distance, shown in full length in a setting. Sometimes called an 'establishing shot' when used to set the scene at the start of the film.
High/low angle	The camera is placed above (high angle) or below (low angle) when filming a character. A high angle can imply smallness, awe or powerlessness; a low angle can show a character dominating or indicate superiority and power.

The choice of camera shot is always deliberate. To discuss this with children, draw their attention to the choice of angle used at certain points in a film (e.g. the beginning, the exciting climax); how different shots are used for different characters; and how certain camera angles can make us feel.

Suggested films: 5 mètres 80 (High Diving Giraffes), France, 2012; *Francis*, UK, 2013.

Sound

We often talk about *seeing a film,* but *listening to a film* might equally be an accurate description. Indeed, sound effects and music can establish the mood of a scene far faster than dialogue or even visual images can. Sound effects and music establish elements of setting (the season, the weather, the time of day), add meaning that might not be obvious from the images, or manipulate the viewer's emotions by suggesting hope or fear. You can ask the children to focus on film-world (diegetic) audible to the characters (footsteps, dialogue, birdsong); or non-film-world (non-diegetic) sounds that have been added in afterwards, such as music or a voiceover.

Children might also be asked to consider why certain pieces of music been chosen for a scene in the film and how this conveys meaning and why moments of silence are included.

Suggested films: El Caminante, UK, 1997; *The Girl and the Fox*, USA, 2011.

Editing and meaning making

Editing is the part of filmmaking where individual film clips – or shots – are joined together to make a longer film. Editing techniques can be used to establish:

- a sense of place (things in the setting);
- time (showing a sequence of events or simultaneous events in different places);
- narrative (what happens and in what order);
- atmosphere.

Editing in a well-made film is largely invisible – how one scene passes into another barely registers with the viewer. Yet understanding even the basic elements of editing can reveal how filmmakers make careful and deliberate choices to manipulate the viewer.

Children can be asked to think about how much time has passed between different shots; how editing and sound are used together; how editing dictates the mood/pace of the film.

Suggested films: Birthday Boy, South Korea, 2004; *Chaperon Rouge*, France, 2006.

Final thoughts on reading film and 21st-century literacy

Learning to read and analyse film is an integral part of becoming literate in the age of widespread digital communication. It can help children understand narrative, inspire their creative responses and validates their personal and cultural experiences. Above all, perhaps, being taught to read film can spark a lifelong love of movies and cinema, reshaping and reaffirming children's identity as readers. Yet the enjoyment and appreciation of film is still to find acceptance as an essential component of literacy teaching in primary schools.

Although the case has been made for the benefits of teaching film, practical problems remain. Even though there exists a vast array of high-quality, short films for children, teachers may be unsure how to seek them out, and many are behind paywalls. While free, good-quality films are available on sites such as *The Literacy Shed,* directors and filmmakers from the Global North – the USA, UK and other European countries – still dominate. There are also practical implications for initial teacher training, ongoing professional development and a broadening of curriculum policy documents – all of which require ambition and vision.

Reading film for pleasure should sit alongside reading books for pleasure as an aspirational target of primary education. Both should be valued, encouraged and celebrated; *cine-* and *vide-literacy* should be recognised as central to how we prepare children for living and thriving in a visual world. This perhaps presents the greatest challenge: instigating a cultural shift in how educators and stakeholders define what it means to be literate in the 21st century.

Having acknowledged that film has a firm place in the development of a love of reading, alongside books and other texts, we will now consider the wider reading environment, and expand on the diverse range of texts that might motivate and inspire children.

Focus on the reading environment

In this section of the chapter, we will reflect on how the classroom and the reading materials chosen, including graphic literature such as comics, encourage children to engage with reading in their environment. We will explore:

- how the meaningful development of the wider reading environment is influential in supporting readers of all ages and stages;
- why the adult role is essential to reading for meaning within any reading environment.

The reading environment

The environment is one of the key features which needs to be effectively planned, implemented and consistently developed to support the ongoing engagement and enthusiasm of readers. When considering reading impact, it is essential to recognise the environment as one of the influential elements in the interaction and exchange of ideas, vocabulary and themes. Chambers' (2011) 'Reading Circle' model effectively demonstrates this. Every time we choose to read, we engage in a series of activities including book choice, response and approach. The reading environment is the cradle which supports this series of choices. As Cremin discussed in Chapter 1, the reading environment is strongly influenced at its core by enthusiastic adults with a knowledge of both classic and contemporary children's literature. Teachers should not only possess an up-to-date knowledge of children's books, but also know the preferences of individual pupils within the class, supporting them effectively by allowing children to access books and to respond to what they have read.

Case study: using comics in the classroom – *The Map comic series*

Why comics?

Comics can change lives. The seamless blending of words and pictures captured in comic form can positively influence all children, but particularly those who have become disengaged or disillusioned with more formal approaches to literacy.

That is not to say that comics do not have a rich cultural history. The two most widely known British comics, *The Beano* and *The Dandy*, were released in the 1930s. By 1950, the weekly circulation of both had reached 2 million. People still talk fondly of reading both titles avidly as a child, consuming page after page in quick succession. Reading comics supported them in their reading journey towards the essential dual skills of automaticity and comprehension. Comics are long enough in duration to be engaging but short enough to be non-threatening, and they allow ample opportunity for children to use them as aerial drones: scanning the past, present and future of a story quickly and easily in each issue.

The value of comics as an effective learning format has long been the subject of debate. In his TED Talk 'Comics belong in the Classroom' (2018), educationalist and comic enthusiast Gene Luen Yang reported that in the 1954 book *The Seduction of the Innocent*, the author and child

→

psychologist Wertham suggested that comics caused juvenile delinquency. The impact of this book resulted in the US Senate holding a series of hearings to see if comics were guilty of this charge. Hearings ended inconclusively, but damaged the reputation of comics in education. For many years, comics were considered disruptive. While many publishers of guided and home reading books now utilise a comic-book style in some instances, only comparatively recently have 'real' comic books and graphic novels been found in the classroom, championed by authors and illustrators such as Neil Gaiman and Chris Riddell.

The Map comic series

The development of *The Map* series came about through the search for materials that linked children's ongoing learning to their school phonics programme. The comics are specifically written for teachers to use and adapt to suit their own needs.

Figure 9.2   Front cover of issue 2, The Map comic series, written by Catherine Lenahan, artwork by Nicolas R Giacondino, self-published.

While initially based on the guidance document *Letters and Sounds* (DfE, 2007), each series can be easily edited to mirror the teaching and progression of any phonics programme. Children are only exposed to the graphemes that they have been taught, allowing confidence and automaticity to develop naturally. Each comic series builds incrementally around four main characters and their adventures. These comics can be used as teaching tools during phonics sessions, as a tool of engagement in reading areas, as home readers. Teachers, understanding the needs of their children, should have the freedom to choose accordingly rather than strictly adhering to any script.

Every comic contains several phonic activities such as word searches, character cards and games. All editions are accompanied by a longer (text only) version of the story which can be read aloud and used for wider class teaching (e.g. vocabulary development and a focus on comprehension).

In short, these scaffolds support children by allowing them to focus in on decoding skills. Effectively, the children already know and comprehend the story prior to decoding. To support this, the illustrations have been designed to 'tell' the story. Where there are children who cannot or do not have access to an engaged adult in the home, the comics attempt to bridge the gap, encouraging fascination and accessibility around graphemes that children have covered in school.

When placed within a quality reading environment alongside a variety of texts, the demand for comics changes the dynamic of the reading experience. When including mainstream comics in a reading area, it is interesting to note the levels of interest, particularly by those boys who had yet to demonstrate phonic acquisition or an interest in books. Their familiarity with characters allowed for enjoyable and often expert conversations with peers; this early exposure to character knowledge allowed a teacher to engage children with linked literacy activities which were friendly and imaginative by default. However, the presentation of text often written in capitals might be a cause for concern for progression.

Comics and graphic literature can add variety to the reading environment. Ongoing EYFS statutory guidance documents identify the two main strands of teaching necessary to support children as beginning readers and writers: engagement and exposure to a wide range of reading materials and the phonological/phonic approach involved in learning sounds and letters. This is continued through into the National Curriculum programmes of study for Key Stages 1 and 2 (DfE, 2013). The two sections consist of word reading and comprehension and there is an acknowledgement that 'different kinds of teaching are needed for each'. Trelease (2013) states that: 'Giving phonics lessons to kids who don't have any print in their lives is like giving oars to people who don't have a boat – you don't get very far' (p107).

For many children, developing the phonics skills involved in learning to read can be long and arduous as they move through the initial one letter–one sound into the demands of digraphs, trigraphs, tricky words and beyond. To succeed in the process of decoding and move towards reading fluency, children must have an end goal in sight – the enjoyment and love of literature and the intrinsic ambition to read independently. To achieve this, beyond the 'code' of phonics, they must have two things: access to engaging books and a reading role model who has repeatedly modelled the processes, engaged in related discussion and demonstrated enjoyment while doing so. This is achievable through consistently immersing children in books (fiction and non-fiction) and poems in many different forms – through guided, shared, reading aloud for pleasure and independent reading.

A well-stocked reading area allows children the benefits of not only personal selection, but also opportunities to share recommendations and responses. As Kozol (2000) maintained: 'Few forms of theft are quite as damaging to inner-city children as the denial of a well-endowed school library' (p96).

Activity: audit your existing book area

Audit your reading area of the classroom you are working in. Are you familiar with books freely available in your classroom and are you confident to recommend them? How do you introduce new books?

Consider shrouding them in mystery and allowing children to deduce the book subject through a series of clues, have them posted or lay out a 'book walk' using key props! A new and unexpected classroom display can also prompt curiosity.

While Kozol (2000) emphasises a school library, this is just as true of a classroom reading area. When choosing a book, most readers will have a specific text type in mind; if a child's text type preference is not available, they are less likely to be sufficiently engaged in reading for a sustained period.

As you gain confidence in developing the reading area in your classroom, you may wish to consider how it complements and contributes to the wider reading environment of the school. Is there clear progression for children as they move between year groups and key stages? Jane Kennedy of Education Durham gives the example of *Beegu, Kensuke's Kingdom* and *Robinson Crusoe* as books with similar themes for children of different age ranges. Exposure to each of these texts would support repeated exposure to similar themes, within increasingly demanding content. Christopher Booker's *The Seven Basic Plots: Why We Tell Stories* (2004) can be a useful aide memoire in developing a network of story areas across a school environment. The plots consist of:

- overcoming the monster
- rags to riches
- the quest
- voyage and return
- comedy
- tragedy
- rebirth.

Activity: stories with similar themes

Work with your school's literacy subject lead to identify stories with similar themes across key stages, ensuring you have appropriate books in your classroom environment. This will support children developing their reading independence and automaticity.

Learning outcomes review

In this chapter you have explored:

- debates around becoming literate in the 21st century;
- some of the rewards of teaching film in primary literacy;
- strategies for teaching children to read a film;
- how the meaningful development of the wider reading environment is influential in supporting readers of all ages and stages;
- why the adult role is essential to reading for meaning within any reading environment.

Conclusion

In this chapter, we have focused on two keys things that have a significant influence on the lives of children: film and a reading environment with a rich variety of texts. These should be valued and encouraged, providing children with variety and diversity of choice. As Cremin noted in Chapter 1, developing children's desire to read is challenging and, although we cannot demand they find pleasure in texts, we can entice and engage them as readers. When considering reading impact, it is essential to recognise the diverse reading environment as one of the influential elements in the development of children's literacy skills and attitudes towards reading and books. We have acknowledged how, in this multimodal era, the inclusion of a diverse range of accessible media such as film, in the reading environment and in our teaching, can develop children's literacy skills and their levels of engagement, influence reading for meaning and contribute to the development of a love of books.

References

Avgerinou, M. (2009) Re-viewing visual literacy in the 'bain d'images' era. *TechTrends*, 53(2): 28–34.

Avgerinou, M. and Ericson, J. (1997) A review of the concept of visual literacy. *British Journal of Educational Technology*, 28(4): 280–91.

Booker, C. (2004) *The Seven Basic Plots: Why We Tell Stories*. London: Bloomsbury.

British Film Institute (BFI) (2000) *Moving Images in the Classroom: A Secondary Teacher's Guide to Using Film and Television*. London: BFI.

British Film Institute (2008) *Film: 21st Century Literacy*. London: BFI.

Buckingham, D. (2015) Defining digital literacy: what do you people need to know about digital media? *Nordic Journal of Digital Literacy*, 2006–2016: 21–34.

Chambers, A. (2011) *Tell Me, Children Reading & Talk with The Reading Environment* (combined volume). Stroud: Thimble Press.

Cope, B. and Kalantzis, M. (2015) *A Pedagogy of Multiliteracies*. London: Palgrave Macmillan.

Davis, N. (2019) Study links high levels of screen time to slower child development. *Guardian*, 28 January. Available at: https://www.theguardian.com/society/2019/jan/28/study-links-high-levels-of-screen-time-to-slower-child-development (accessed 1 May 2020).

Department for Education (DfE) (2007) *Letters and Sounds*. London: DfE.

Department for Education (2011) *Teachers' Standards in England from September 2012*. London: DfE.

Department for Education (DfE) (2013) *The National Curriculum in England: Key Stages 1 and 2 Framework Document*. London: DfE.

Department for Education (2014) *National Curriculum: Programmes of Study for English*. London: DfE.

Department for Education (2107) *Statutory Framework for the Early Years Foundation Stage*. London; DfE.

Kozol, J. (2000) An unequal education. *School Library Journal*, 46(5): 46–9.

Kucharczyk, S. (2016) *Engaging Your Rogue Ones: Bringing Star Wars into the Classroom*. Available at: https://www.tes.com/blog/engaging-your-rogue-ones-bringing-star-wars-classroom (accessed 1 May 2020).

Lundy, A. and Stephens, A. (2015) Beyond the literal: teaching visual literacy in the 21st century classroom. *Procedia: Social and Behavioral Sciences*, 174: 1057–60.

National Council of Teachers of English (NCTE) (2019) *Definition of Literacy in a Digital Age*. Available at: https://ncte.org/statement/nctes-definition-literacy-digital-age (accessed 1 May 2020).

National Literacy Trust (NLT) (2020) *Children and Young People's Reading in 2019: Findings from our Annual Literacy Survey*. Available at: https://cdn.literacytrust.org.uk/media/documents/Reading_trends_in_2019_-_Final.pdf (accessed 1 May 2020).

New London Group (1996) A pedagogy of multiliteracies: designing social futures. *Harvard Educational Review*, 66(1): 60–93.

Pantaleo, S. (2015) Language, literacy and visual texts. *English in Education*, 49(2): 113–29.

Parker, D. (1999) You've read the book, now make the film: moving image media, print literacy and narrative. *English in Education*, 33(1): 24–35.

Parry, B. (2013) *Children, Film and Literacy*. Basingstoke: Palgrave Macmillan.

Parry, B. with Bulman, J.H. (2017) *Film Education, Literacy and Learning*. Leicester: UKLA.

Smidt, S. (2010) *Playing to Learn: The Role of Play in the Early Years*. Oxford: Routledge.

Trelease, J. (2013) *The Read-Aloud Handbook* (7th edn). London: Penguin.

United Nations Education Science and Cultural Organisation (UNESCO) (2015) *The Futures of Learning 2: What Kind of Learning for the 21st Century?* Available at: https://unesdoc.unesco.org/ark:/48223/pf0000242996 (accessed 1 May 2020).

Wertham, F. (1954) *The Seduction of the Innocent*. New York: Rinehart & Co.

10 Conclusion: What Can I Do Now?

Angela Gill, Megan Stephenson and David Waugh

When considering how to develop a love of reading, this book has identified what trainee teachers and early career teachers can do to develop their own teaching and learning and classroom environment. This book has illustrated not only the value of reading for pleasure, but also the ways in which a culture of reading for pleasure can be developed.

This chapter provides ideas about what you might consider now, reflected in your own practice. The chapter begins with some ideas about how you might develop a culture of reading in your teaching environment. Later in the chapter, top tips for teaching are provided by our authors, indicating how you can implement the ideas they describe in their chapters. These are accompanied by recommendations by our authors for further reading, children's texts, websites and high-quality resources.

Developing a culture of reading for pleasure: continuing to promote a reading environment at classroom and school level

Giving space, time and high status to reading determines that 'reading matters' in school. Therefore, it is important that time is set aside for pupils to read for pleasure. Establishing a culture of valuing resources and respecting these areas is essential. Such a philosophy begins initially in Early Years provision (see Chapter 2) and then develops into KS1 and beyond (see Chapter 3). Jolliffe and Waugh (2018) emphasise the need for this to be whole-school led so that all classes are expected to have quality provision within reading environments (such as reading corners) and common conventions, leading to the establishment of common goals and a whole-school approach of a love of reading. As Teresa Cremin noted in Chapter 1: 'We cannot demand they find pleasure in texts, but we can entice and engage them as readers, and create relaxed invitational spaces in which book talk is valued.'

The designation of English Hub schools has provided 'Beacons' or '*Islets of Expertise*' where best practice is displayed for others during continual professional development sessions. Ideas can at this time be 'magpied' when visiting such areas of excellence, cascading best practice and ultimately developing this into a wider number of settings. Below is a list of ideas to support schools in developing a whole-school approach to encouraging reading for pleasure. Consider how you might use these in your own teaching environment.

Reading areas supplied and regularly updated that include:

Topical and current texts, a range of fiction/non-fiction and a range of styles.

Giving ownership to pupils to respect and look after the area.

Including where possible eBook readers and other alternative forms of screen reading.

Reading buddies:

Mixing age phases and reading abilities across school provides excellent opportunities for pupils to get to know others and share best reading practice.

Regular opportunities to complete book reviews and blogs:

Using the school website to write about current books and 'share' preferences is a more accessible and current form of book reviewing.

This also makes the reporting available to parents and carers – vital so they can read what books the children are reading at school.

Establishing book clubs:

Sets of books that pupils can share in smaller groups and exchange works in a book club. Encouraging older pupils to organise and monitor this also provides opportunities for mixed age phases to get together and discuss their varying preferences.

Reading events:

Inviting authors in to speak about their books.

Displaying texts, extracts and reviews around school and in shared spaces.

'Bring and share' small pop-up libraries across the year.

Reading communities and school libraries:

Alongside these ideas it is accepted that most schools will have a library. However, access to this needs to be organised centrally. Resources needn't be endless, and communities can be asked to help 'top up' books by sending in 'preloved' materials that children no longer wish to read at home. Many teachers themselves will supply resources from their own children's 'stocks' – although this should not be relied upon as a resource stream. Community libraries will also supply books that are no longer being loaned regularly by members. However, in recent years public funding for local libraries has meant many schools now rely on their own community for support here. Giving children a level of responsibility to look after the loans and the library area in school also promotes a positive independent environment.

Involving parents in promoting a reading culture:

This can be challenging but rewarding and is essential if the culture is to be embedded.

The impact on parental involvement, parental support and family education should never be underestimated. Parents should always be encouraged to be actively involved in monitoring pupils' independent reading (Gamble, 2019, p310). Goodall and Montgomery (2014) point out the need for schools to balance parents' support of reading instruction and that of engagement. They warn schools should not make judgements about parental involvement. Schools can and should encourage parental involvement and engagement by promoting both reading instruction and independence, through the curriculum and reading for pleasure as a continuum. Termly newsletters that identify books being used to teach the reading and promote reading for pleasure are a good opportunity alongside publicity surrounding different reading for pleasure initiatives, providing parents with the knowledge of what schools are doing but also how parents can get involved and encourage children to read for pleasure.

Celebrating reading – beyond stickers:

Most schools will promote and celebrate children who read regularly for instruction and for pleasure. However, more recently many teachers have stretched this level of celebration beyond the norms of a 'well done' sticker. Examples can be seen in rewards for 'extreme' readers, where pupils take photos of themselves reading outdoors or in unusual places. These photos are displayed in whole-school assemblies and book vouchers given to those who contribute. Tweeting book reviews in a limited number of words is also a challenge some schools have recommended to their pupils. Here, pupils are encouraged to group together or send in separate reviews of a book they have read for pleasure in no more than twenty words.

Top tips for teaching and recommended resources from our authors

In Chapter 1, about building communities of engaged readers, Teresa Cremin argued that enjoyment in reading is central to the culture and ethos of the classroom and will be sustained by interactive and reciprocal reader relationships. The vital importance of teachers being readers themselves with a good knowledge of texts is emphasised in a chapter which describes the key features of reading for pleasure communities. See Teresa's top tips on the next page.

TOP TIPS FOR TEACHING

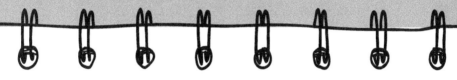

- ☐ Develop your professional knowledge of children's texts.

- ☐ Get to know your readers, their interest and identities.

- ☐ Develop a research informed RfP pedagogy.

- ☐ Enrich your practice through becoming a Reading Teacher: a teacher who reads and a reader who teaches.

- ☐ Build reading communities which are interactive and reciprocal, based on the points above.

RECOMMENDED TEXTS AND OTHER RESOURCES

Books for Topics: Collates booklists to help teachers
find and use quality texts in the classroom
and on their own reading journeys.
https://www.booksfortopics.com/

Book Award Winners: A summary of all
children's book award winners each year.
https://www.researchrichpedagogies.org/
news-awards/details/book-award-winners-2018-19

Books for Keeps: This independent children's
book magazine reviews hundreds of new children's
books each year and publishes articles on
every aspect of writing for children.
http://booksforkeeps.co.uk/

Chambers, A.
(2011) *Tell Me, Children Reading & Talk with
The Reading Environment* (combined volume).
Stroud: Thimble Press.

Cremin, T., Mottram, M.,
Powell, S., Collins, R. and Safford, K.
(2014) *Building Communities of Engaged Readers:
Reading for Pleasure.* London and NY: Routledge.

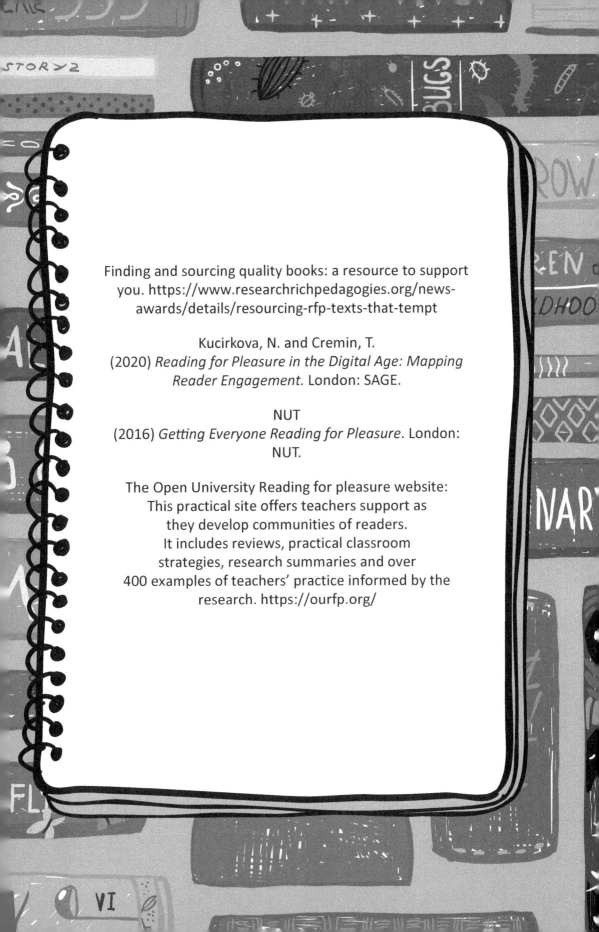

Finding and sourcing quality books: a resource to support you. https://www.researchrichpedagogies.org/news-awards/details/resourcing-rfp-texts-that-tempt

Kucirkova, N. and Cremin, T.
(2020) *Reading for Pleasure in the Digital Age: Mapping Reader Engagement.* London: SAGE.

NUT
(2016) *Getting Everyone Reading for Pleasure*. London: NUT.

The Open University Reading for pleasure website: This practical site offers teachers support as they develop communities of readers. It includes reviews, practical classroom strategies, research summaries and over 400 examples of teachers' practice informed by the research. https://ourfp.org/

In Chapter 2, about supporting children to enjoy reading in EYFS and KS1, Cathy Lawson, Sam Wilkes and Megan Stephenson explored how the demands of a curriculum-heavy content can be met through the creative planning, teaching and delivery of engaging material. The authors considered how instructional teaching of systematic synthetic phonics (SSP) can be expertly balanced with the introduction of high-quality texts that engage children and help develop a culture of and a thirst for reading.

TOP TIPS FOR TEACHING

☐ Immerse children in spoken language and books as early as possible.

☐ Balancing out your approach: discrete teaching of phonics and the use of whole books are essential if children are to learn to read and are to read for pleasure.

☐ Reflect on the texts you use: there is room for traditional authors and new writers in the curriculum.

☐ Keep current: look out for new and inclusive texts all the time. Children need to see themselves reflected in the books they read.

☐ Work collegiately: whole-school approaches are essential. Get parents and communities involved.

RECOMMENDED TEXTS AND OTHER RESOURCES

WEBSITES

There are many supportive and encouraging web materials for both teachers and parents.

This website is an excellent source of information and includes free online extracts for children:
The Reading Agency. https://readingagency.org.uk/

Oxford Owl.
https://www.oxfordowl.co.uk/

Just Imagine's Ear For Reading.
https://justimagine.co.uk/

The Reading Journey.
https://www.thereadingjourney.co.uk/

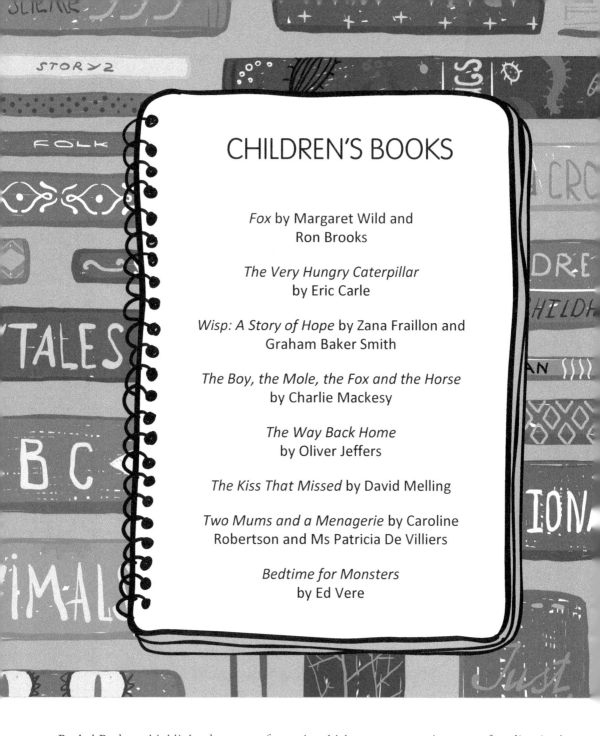

CHILDREN'S BOOKS

Fox by Margaret Wild and
Ron Brooks

The Very Hungry Caterpillar
by Eric Carle

Wisp: A Story of Hope by Zana Fraillon and
Graham Baker Smith

The Boy, the Mole, the Fox and the Horse
by Charlie Mackesy

The Way Back Home
by Oliver Jeffers

The Kiss That Missed by David Melling

Two Mums and a Menagerie by Caroline
Robertson and Ms Patricia De Villiers

Bedtime for Monsters
by Ed Vere

Rachel Rudman highlighted a range of ways in which to promote enjoyment of reading in the classroom and beyond in Chapter 3, about supporting developing readers to thrive through KS2 into KS3. Rachel explored ways in which children's reading can be nurtured through the use of challenging texts as they move into upper Key Stage 2 and looked at how a reading culture can be preserved in the transition from primary to secondary school. Rachel's top tips on the next page.

TOP TIPS FOR TEACHING

- [ ] Read widely! As teachers, we have a responsibility to advocate reading widely and for pleasure so we need to do it ourselves and be able to talk about the books we are reading and why we have enjoyed them. It helps if you can provide suggestions for students too.

- [ ] Identify ways to enable children to respond individually to the texts they encounter before being given a perspective or lens through which to view the text. This might be as simple as asking them to write down one or two questions on a sticky note which they would like to know the answers to about the text they are reading. It is important that children feel that their viewpoints are valued and that there is no 'wrong' answer when probing and exploring a text.

- [ ] Look for opportunities to widen children's involvement in reading-related activities. Could they enter competitions to review books or are there book readings taking place at local bookshops?

- [ ] If possible, let children have a say in choosing the class fiction text. Allowing some element of choice encourages greater engagement and buy-in.

- [ ] Become confident in the different domains which are assessed at Key Stage 2. Asking questions which focus on all of these domains will ensure a varied approach to texts which also enables children to approach future tests with confidence.

RECOMMENDED TEXTS AND OTHER RESOURCES

In this short film, Professor Teresa Cremin and teacher Becky Thomson explain the implications of the findings that teachers who share their own experiences of reading make a positive impact on children's desire to read and frequency of reading at home and at school.

Open University Research Rich Pedagogies:

https://researchrichpedagogies.org/research/theme/reading-teachers-teachers-who-read-and-readers-who-teach

CHILDREN'S TEXTS

The Boy at the Back of the Class by Onjali Q. Rauf

Goldfish by Nat Luurtsema

The Curious Incident of the Dog in the Nighttime by Mark Haddon

Carrie's War by Nina Bawden

Goodnight Mr Tom by Michelle Magorian

Holes by Louis Sachar

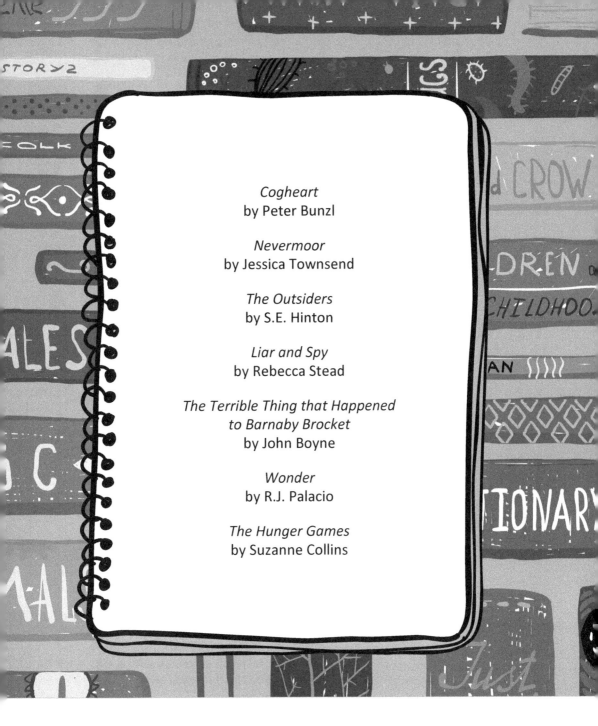

Cogheart
by Peter Bunzl

Nevermoor
by Jessica Townsend

The Outsiders
by S.E. Hinton

Liar and Spy
by Rebecca Stead

*The Terrible Thing that Happened
to Barnaby Brocket*
by John Boyne

Wonder
by R.J. Palacio

The Hunger Games
by Suzanne Collins

In Chapter 4, about the creative curriculum, Lucy Davies argued that cross-curricular texts can not only develop children's subject-specific knowledge, but also their sense of individual and collective identity. Lucy maintained that literature can provide a safe and sensitive stimulus to discuss emotive topics, particularly in history, religious education and citizenship. The themes of 'creative reading' and 'critical reading' were examined and Lucy demonstrated how art and humanities subjects provide a context for enhancing different types of reading skills. See Lucy's top tips overleaf.

TOP TIPS FOR TEACHING

- [ ] Plan ahead as much as possible; this will give you time to start thinking about the best types of reading skills to develop in each topic. It will also give you time to look out for interesting texts and potential venues for visits.

- [ ] Make the most of social media. There are numerous support groups on Facebook for art and humanities co-ordinators. If you are a subject leader, joining these can be a useful way to share ideas and gain knowledge of useful resources and books.

- [ ] Which subjects and topics are you least confident in teaching? Good subject knowledge helps when delivering cross-curricular reading activities. Developing your knowledge in art and the humanities can be enjoyable; visiting art galleries and museums can be good starting points. Many have made resources and virtual tours available on their websites.

- [ ] Refer to the Programme of Study for each subject to ensure that you are meeting their aims as well as improving children's reading skills.

- [ ] Don't be afraid to take risks. Many of the books suggested in this chapter are new and require you to think of lesson ideas and series of lessons yourself, rather than relying on mass-produced lesson plans, or colleagues' 'tried and tested' plans. However, they provide an exciting opportunity to deliver lessons which are relevant to your pupils.

BOOKS AND WEBSITES FOR ART

Bird, M. (2018)
*Vincent's Starry Night and Other Stories:
A Children's History of Art.*
London: Laurence King.

Blake, Q.
(2018) *Tell Me a Picture*.
London: Frances Lincoln.

Hockney, D.
(2018) *A History of Pictures for Children*.
London: Thames & Hudson.

National Society for Education in Art and Design.
https://www.nsead.org/

Tate Britain Kids.
https://www.tate.org.uk/kids?gclid=EAIaIQobCh
MIuvvtmajI6gIVU-3tCh39HgjJEAAYASAAEgIo5fD_BwE

BOOKS AND WEBSITES FOR GEOGRAPHY

Camerini, V.
(2019) *Greta's Story: The Schoolgirl Who Went On Strike to Save the Planet* (2nd edn). London: Simon & Schuster.

Laird, E.
(2018) *Song of the Dolphin Boy*. London: Macmillan.

Weiss, S.
(2020) *Amazing Islands.* London: What on Earth.

Mini-Map Makers.
https://minimapmakers.co.uk/

Geocaching app.
https://www.geocaching.com/play

Digi Maps.
https://digimapforschools.edina.ac.uk/

BOOKS AND WEBSITES FOR HISTORY

McEwan, E.
(2004) *Rose Blanche*. London: Red Fox.

Robinson, M.
(2014) *How to Wash a Woolly Mammoth*.
London: Simon & Schuster.

History Rocks.
https://www.history-rocks.com/

Mr T Does Primary History.
https://www.mrtdoeshistory.com/

BOOKS AND WEBSITES
FOR CITIZENSHIP

Amson-Bradshaw, G.
(2020) *We're All Equal (I'm a Global Citizen)*.
London: Franklin Watts.

Burnell, C.
(2020) *I Am Not a Label: 34 Disabled Artists,
Thinkers, Athletes and Activists from Past and Present*.
London: Wide Eyed Editions.

Foreman, M.
(2013) *Newspaper Boy and Origami Girl*.
London: Anderson Press.

McCloud, C.
(2016) *Have You Filled a Bucket Today?*
(10th anniversary edn). Chicago: Bucket Fillers.

Educate and Celebrate.
https://www.educateandcelebrate.org/
prideineducation/

In Chapter 5, Steve Higgins, Fay Lewis, Rachel Simpson, Jo Smith and David Whitehead maintained that using stories within science, technology, engineering and mathematics (STEM) can both encourage the act of reading and inspire pupils to improve their knowledge about scientific phenomena, the world of technology and mathematics.

TOP TIPS FOR TEACHING

☐ Read lots of children's story books!

☐ Collect lists of books or references to fiction and non-fiction texts which will support your teaching of reading and STEM subjects.

☐ Identify activities which you could develop from these texts for different year groups.

☐ Make sure there are opportunities for children to use the language and vocabulary actively through talking in the classroom.

☐ Make it challenging but fun!

RECOMMENDED TEXTS AND OTHER RESOURCES

BOOKS

Hiebert, E.H. and Sailors, M. (eds)
Finding the Right Texts: What Works for Beginning and Struggling Readers.
New York: Guilford Press, pp89–108.

Mallett, M.
(2019) *Choosing and Using Fiction and Non-Fiction 3–11: A Comprehensive Guide for Teachers and Student Teachers*.
London: Routledge.

Dreher, M.J. and Kletzien, S.B.
(2015) *Teaching Informational Text in K-3 Classrooms: Best Practices to Help Children Read, Write, and Learn from Nonfiction*. New York: Guilford.

Pottle, J. and Smith, C.
(2015) *Science Through Stories*.
Storytelling School Series. Stroud: Hawthorn Press.

Rees, J.
(2019) *Exploring Maths Through Stories and Rhymes: Active Learning in the Early Years*.
London: Routledge.

WEBSITES

Teaching Science Through Stories.
https://www.stem.org.uk/teaching-science-through-stories

MathsThroughStories.org is an international research-based initiative, based in the UK.
https://www.mathsthroughstories.org

Enchanted Learning have over 35,000 pages on a wide range of topics.
https://www.enchantedlearning.com/ELS.shtml

In Chapter 6, about developing a love of language for performance through poetry and drama, Christina Castling and Charlotte Wright argued that drama and poetry can bring language to life in the classroom and show our pupils how its power can be explored and enjoyed in a range of ways. They discussed ways to create a safe and affirmative classroom where children feel happy to perform, as well as how you can build your confidence in helping your pupils to explore the spoken word through poetry and drama.

TOP TIPS FOR TEACHING

☐ Take time to listen to children's use of language in the playground to gain insight into how they already naturally engage in word play and performance.

☐ Build from small moments of performance in the classroom to larger ones with wider audiences.

☐ Be bold in actively seeking out opportunities to get the children up on their feet and exploring words experientially and playfully.

☐ Create shared rules and expectations for performance to help everyone feel safe to participate in the classroom.

☐ Model an enthusiasm for creating and finding texts for spoken performance, showing that confidence can be increased by 'having a go'.

CHILDREN'S TEXTS

You Tell Me
by Michael Rosen and Roger McGough

Poems to Perform: A Classic Collection
by Julia Donaldson

Heard it in the Playground/Please Mrs Butler
by Allan Ahlberg

The Rainmaker Danced
by John Agard

Revolting Rhymes
by Roald Dahl

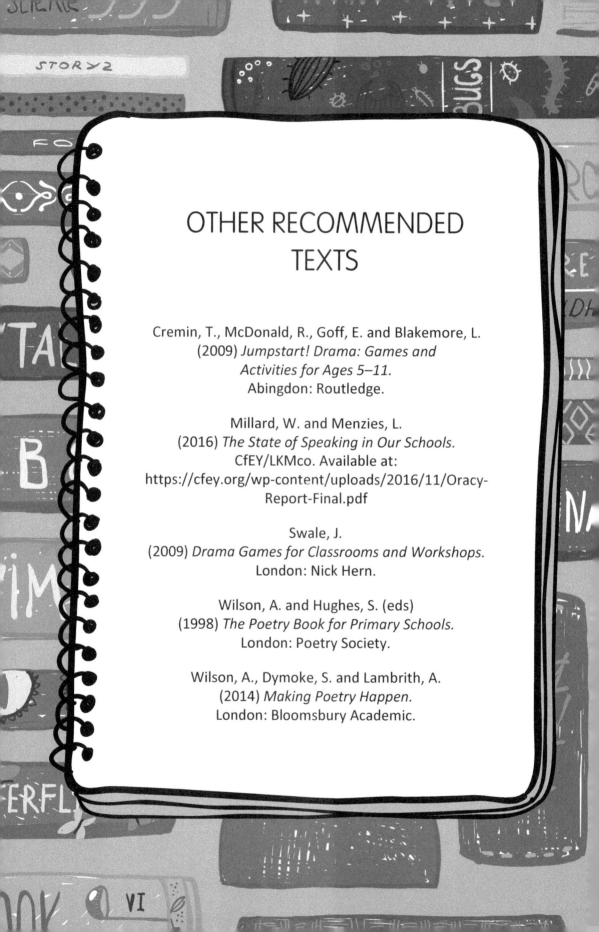

OTHER RECOMMENDED TEXTS

Cremin, T., McDonald, R., Goff, E. and Blakemore, L.
(2009) *Jumpstart! Drama: Games and
Activities for Ages 5–11.*
Abingdon: Routledge.

Millard, W. and Menzies, L.
(2016) *The State of Speaking in Our Schools.*
CfEY/LKMco. Available at:
https://cfey.org/wp-content/uploads/2016/11/Oracy-
Report-Final.pdf

Swale, J.
(2009) *Drama Games for Classrooms and Workshops.*
London: Nick Hern.

Wilson, A. and Hughes, S. (eds)
(1998) *The Poetry Book for Primary Schools.*
London: Poetry Society.

Wilson, A., Dymoke, S. and Lambrith, A.
(2014) *Making Poetry Happen.*
London: Bloomsbury Academic.

Diana Mann and Amanda Nuttall suggested, in Chapter 7 about building diversity and inclusion through high-quality texts, that books could be our most powerful tool for building diversity, inclusion and acceptance in our classrooms. They maintained that we have a responsibility to think carefully about the books we share with our children, ensuring authentic representation of a range of diverse, multidimensional characters, including those which challenge stereotypes and normalise difference.

TOP TIPS FOR TEACHING

- [ ] Select books in which the characters have distinct personalities regardless of their gender, race, sexuality or ability.

- [ ] Make a conscious effort to select books for children that reflect fairness and inspire both genders.

- [ ] Select books that show under-represented groups in roles such as scientists, explorers, adventurers, promoting strong and successful role models for everyone.

- [ ] Ensure that there are also books that offer realistic and engaging stories that represent issues of diversity in an age-appropriate way.

- [ ] Ask community members and parents/carers to suggest their favourite childhood stories, authors and texts, to include those which reflect diverse cultures and lived experiences (although these may need to be evaluated).

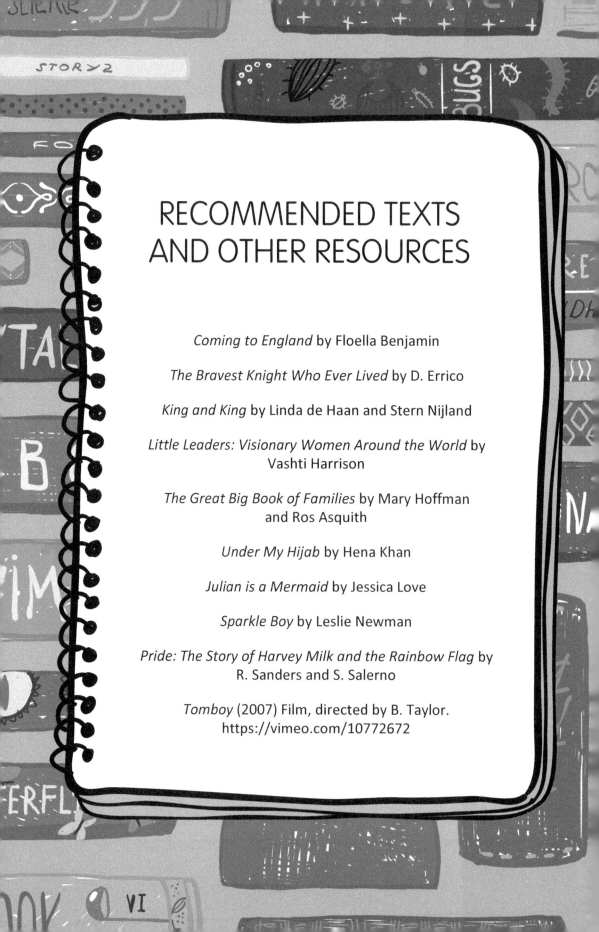

RECOMMENDED TEXTS AND OTHER RESOURCES

Coming to England by Floella Benjamin

The Bravest Knight Who Ever Lived by D. Errico

King and King by Linda de Haan and Stern Nijland

Little Leaders: Visionary Women Around the World by Vashti Harrison

The Great Big Book of Families by Mary Hoffman and Ros Asquith

Under My Hijab by Hena Khan

Julian is a Mermaid by Jessica Love

Sparkle Boy by Leslie Newman

Pride: The Story of Harvey Milk and the Rainbow Flag by R. Sanders and S. Salerno

Tomboy (2007) Film, directed by B. Taylor.
https://vimeo.com/10772672

Kulwinder Maude, in Chapter 8 about deeper reading for EAL pupils, argued that as more and more teachers find themselves teaching students from increasingly diverse linguistic and cultural backgrounds, it is vital that ESOL pupils are given opportunities to engage with language through meaningful contexts where they can refine their initial thoughts through classroom talk.

TOP TIPS FOR TEACHING

- ☐ Build vocabulary in the second language by engaging in extensive reading.

- ☐ Encourage engagement with public or school libraries.

- ☐ Inspire EAL pupils to read books they are really interested in.

- ☐ Normalise the use of first language in the classroom.

- ☐ Invest in dual language books (see mantralingua.com).

RECOMMENDED TEXTS

Conteh, J.
(2012a) Language diversity and 'English as an additional language' (EAL) in the UK: issues for teacher education, in E. Winters-Ohle, B. Seipp and B. Ralle (eds), *Lehrer für schüler mit migrationsgeschichte: sprachliche kompetenz in kintext internationaler konzepte der lehrerbildung.* Münster: Waxmann, pp130–8, 227–32.

Conteh, J.
(2012b) *Teaching Bilingual and EAL Learners in Primary Schools: Transforming Primary QTS.* London: SAGE.

Conteh, J.
(2013) Multilingual literacies in mainstream classroom contexts, in D. Martin (ed.), *Researching Dyslexia in Multilingual Settings: Diverse Perspectives.* Clevedon: Multilingual Matters.

Flynn, N.
(2013) Linguistic capital and the linguistic field for teachers unaccustomed to linguistic difference. *British Journal of Sociology of Education*, 34(2): 225–42. doi: https://doi.org/10.1080/01425692.2012.710004

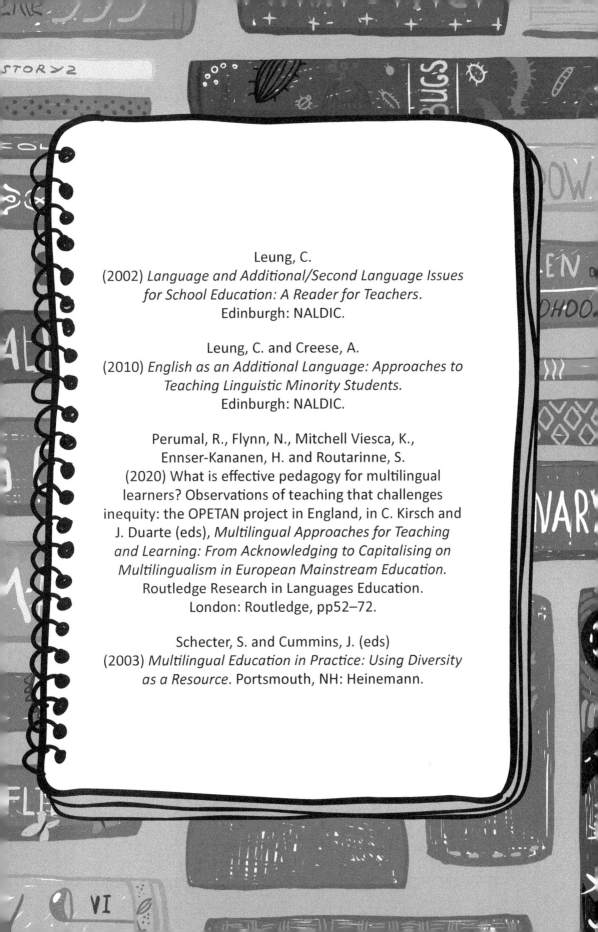

Leung, C.
(2002) *Language and Additional/Second Language Issues for School Education: A Reader for Teachers.*
Edinburgh: NALDIC.

Leung, C. and Creese, A.
(2010) *English as an Additional Language: Approaches to Teaching Linguistic Minority Students.*
Edinburgh: NALDIC.

Perumal, R., Flynn, N., Mitchell Viesca, K., Ennser-Kananen, H. and Routarinne, S.
(2020) What is effective pedagogy for multilingual learners? Observations of teaching that challenges inequity: the OPETAN project in England, in C. Kirsch and J. Duarte (eds), *Multilingual Approaches for Teaching and Learning: From Acknowledging to Capitalising on Multilingualism in European Mainstream Education.*
Routledge Research in Languages Education.
London: Routledge, pp52–72.

Schecter, S. and Cummins, J. (eds)
(2003) *Multilingual Education in Practice: Using Diversity as a Resource.* Portsmouth, NH: Heinemann.

In Chapter 9, about the diverse reading environment, Angela Gill, Stefan Kucharczyk and Catherine Lenahan considered what it means to become literate in the 21st century and how the texts we encounter may go beyond books. Angela, Stefan and Catherine maintained that in a multimodal era the inclusion of a diverse range of accessible media, such as film, in the reading environment and in our teaching can develop children's literacy skills and their levels of engagement, influence reading for meaning and contribute to the development of a love of books. The authors also demonstrated why the adult role is essential to reading for meaning within any reading environment.

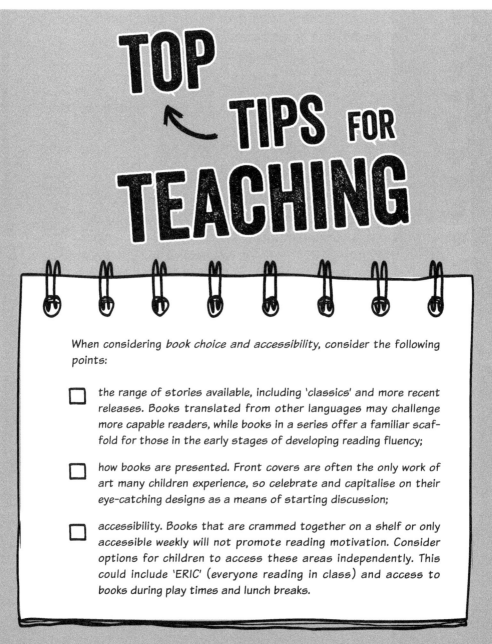

TOP TIPS FOR TEACHING

When considering *book choice and accessibility*, consider the following points:

- ☐ the range of stories available, including 'classics' and more recent releases. Books translated from other languages may challenge more capable readers, while books in a series offer a familiar scaffold for those in the early stages of developing reading fluency;

- ☐ how books are presented. Front covers are often the only work of art many children experience, so celebrate and capitalise on their eye-catching designs as a means of starting discussion;

- ☐ accessibility. Books that are crammed together on a shelf or only accessible weekly will not promote reading motivation. Consider options for children to access these areas independently. This could include 'ERIC' (everyone reading in class) and access to books during play times and lunch breaks.

TOP TIPS FOR TEACHING

When considering the *timings of the reading day* and opportunities for children to access reading materials, consider:

- [ ] that the time available for children to access these resources is vital. A once-a-week 'treat' or, even worse, a 'reward' for finishing work early will not support those children who really need the experiences great stories can offer. Little and often is the order of the day;

- [ ] an opportunity to enjoy a personal sustained reading time with a book that does not come from a prescribed list. Phonically decodable books can be great at building word recognition and fluency skills when those books are closely matched to what they have been taught, but these books may not match the passions of the children reading them. Experiment and expose children to a rich variety of literature.

When supporting *book-related discussion*, you may like to discuss the following with more experienced educators.

- [ ] How do you facilitate opportunities to chat about and recommend books either with peers or adults in the classroom?

- [ ] How do you support opportunities to hear books read aloud by a variety of readers? Some books are more effectively read by one person than another. A visit from an author or illustrator may not be possible, but your secretary, caretaker or an enthusiastic grandparent can often be inspiring too. All of these people can support with their own personal point of view, which may prompt a new direction in discussion.

- [ ] How do you make books areas look enticing and 'chat-worthy'? Keeping things up to date and engaging must be managed as part of an already busy schedule. Are children involved in this preparation?

RECOMMENDED TEXTS AND OTHER RESOURCES

CHILDREN'S TEXTS

The Girl Who Loved Wellies by Zehra Hicks

Peck, Peck, Peck by Lucy Cousins

The Adventures of Dish and Spoon by Mini Grey

Beegu by Alexis Deacon

Extra Yarn by Mac Barnett

Beast Quest series by Adam Blade

Rainbow Fairies series by Daisy Meadows

The Canterville Ghost by Oscar Wilde

Arabian Nights translated by Brian Alderson

The Map comic series by Catherine Lenahan

WEB RESOURCES

In addition to films available on DVD or streaming, quality short films designed for primary-age viewers can be accessed for free at the Literacy Shed website (www.literacyshed.co.uk) and the British Film Institute (BFI) website (https://player.bfi.org.uk/free).

www.booktrust.org.uk

https://literacytrust.org.uk/primary/

www.educationendowmentfoundation.org.uk

BOOKS AND RESOURCES
FOR READING FILM AND 21ST-CENTURY LITERACY

Information on film and practical teaching ideas can be found in the following:

Parry, B. with Bulman, J.H.
(2017) *Film Education, Literacy and Learning.*
Leicester: UKLA.

Roberts, G. and Wallis, H.
(2001) *Introducing Film.* London: Arnold.

Stafford, T.
(2011) *Teaching Visual Literacy in the Primary Classroom: Comic Books, Films, Television and Picture Narratives.*
Oxford: Routledge.

FOR THE READING ENVIRONMENT

Chambers, A.
(2011) *Tell Me, Children Reading & Talk with The Reading Environment* (combined volume).
Stroud: Thimble Press.

Eccleshare, J.
(2019) *1001 Children's Books You Must Read Before You Grow Up.*
London: Cassell.

Horst, J., Flack, Z. and Lenahan, C.
(2017) *Policy Brief: Benefits of Repeated Reading with EYFS Children.*
Brighton: University of Sussex.

We hope that now you have read this book you will be stimulated to develop your knowledge and understanding of children's literature, including poetry, plays and multimodal texts. We hope, too, that you will recognise the importance of developing a reading for pleasure culture in your teaching environment and beyond, sharing your own enthusiasm for reading with the children you teach.

Angela Gill
Megan Stephenson
David Waugh
March 2021

References

Gamble, N. (2019) *Exploring Children's Literature: Reading Knowledge, Understanding and Pleasure* (4th edn). London: SAGE.

Goodall, J. and Montgomery, C. (2014) Parental involvement to parental engagement: a continuum. *Education Review*, 66(4): 399–410.

Jolliffe, W. and Waugh, D. (2018) *Mastering Primary English*. London: Bloomsbury.

Index